Artist-Entrepreneurs

Saint Gaudens, MacMonnies, and Parrish

Dianne Durante

2019

Copyright, Credits, Acknowledgments

COVER

Cover design by Allegra Durante https://www.AllegraDurante.com/contact/ . Cover images: MacMonnies's *Hale* and Saint Gaudens's *Sherman*: Photos copyright © 2019 Dianne L. Durante. Parrish's *Griselda*: Wikipedia. Saint Gaudens's *Lincoln*: AndrewHorne / Wikipedia.

ACKNOWLEDGMENTS

Many thanks to the New York Objectivist Club for sponsoring the original "Artist-Entrepreneurs" talk in 1998, and to Quent and Linda Cordair of Quent Cordair Fine Art (www.Cordair.com) for giving me the opportunity to offer an updated version of the talk in Napa in 2018.

Thanks to Jeri Egan, John Cerasuolo, Brian Lessing, Stacy Peterson, Bruce Van Horne, Tom Lauerman, Jay & Joan Conne, Adrina & Milton Cohen, Heather Blease, Stacey Hoffman, and Jerome Wilson for their support of the publication of this book. Special thanks to Adam Reed, E.M. Allison, and Duncan Curry, who have supported my work with recurring payments via the highest tiers on Patreon, and now via the Tip Jar on DianneDuranteWriter.com. To support my work, visit https://diannedurantewriter.com/sunday-recommendations/ .

As always, thanks to my sister Jan Robinson for her meticulous proofreading. Any errors that remain are my own responsibility.

First published 8/9/2019 via Amazon.

This issue published 10/23/2022.

Table of Contents

Introduction

When I start researching a new project, there's always a giddy period when I read massive amounts and search for every possible related image. It's selfish fun to gather and sort and integrate all that data. But eventually, if I'm planning to share the knowledge with others (another selfish pleasure!), I have to settle down and decide what point I want to make.

The point I decided to make in this book was that Saint Gaudens, MacMonnies, and Parrish were not only great artists, but great businessmen. They produced beautiful, innovative works, and they were also hard-working and profit-minded.

The eldest of the three was Augustus Saint Gaudens. (He pronounced it "GAWdenz".) Saint Gaudens was the son of poor immigrants. By his thirties, he was one of America's best and most famous sculptors. From 1880 to 1907, he created thirty-five important public monuments and dozens of smaller works, all of them carefully thought out and original.

Our second artist is Frederick MacMonnies. Fifteen years younger than Saint Gaudens, he was another talented sculptor who produced inspiring work and profited from it. In the mid-1890s, his annual income was about $300,000—more than $7.5 million in 2019 dollars.

1850s | 1860s | 1870s | 1880s | 1890s | 1900s | 1910s | 1920s | 1930s | 1940s | 1950s | 1960s

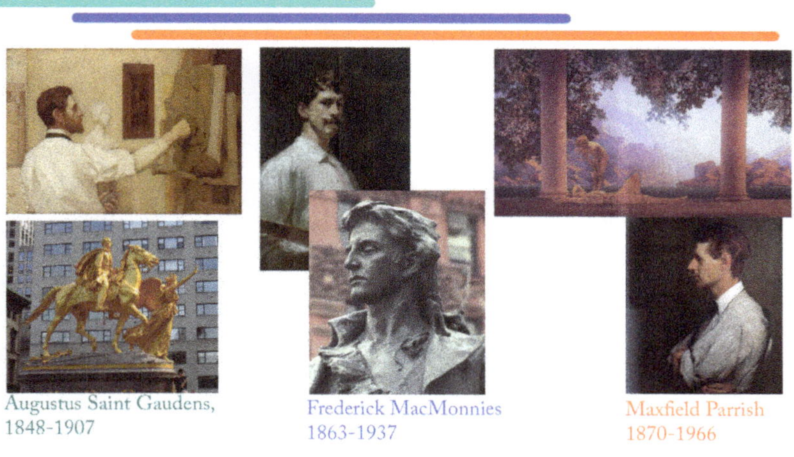

Augustus Saint Gaudens,
1848-1907

Frederick MacMonnies
1863-1937

Maxfield Parrish
1870-1966

Illustration 1

But MacMonnies's story has a very different ending from Saint Gaudens's, partly due to his personality and partly due to his times.

Our third artist is Maxfield Parrish. Parrish was twenty-two years younger than Saint Gaudens. Like Saint Gaudens and MacMonnies, he worked to learn his craft, developed a distinctive style, and earned a substantial income. In the early 1920s, one out of every four homes in the United States had a print of Parrish's *Daybreak*.

In this book, we'll first glance at the historical and artistic context of the 1880s to 1910s, when Saint Gaudens, MacMonnies, and Parrish were all at work. Then we'll look at each of the three artists: their lives, how they learned their skills, some of their major works, how they became wealthy, and what was distinctive and innovative about their works and their style.

CHAPTER 1
Context

THE STATE OF AMERICA CIRCA 1880-1910

The Civil War ended in 1865, with 600,000 Americans dead: some 2.5% of the population—mostly young men. Saint Gaudens was old enough to remember seeing Lincoln as a teenager, but not old enough to fight in the war. MacMonnies and Parrish didn't live through a major conflict until the United States entered World War I in 1917. There were plenty of horrible ways to die in the late nineteenth century, of course, but when these men were young, they had no images of massive death and destruction burned into their brains from newspapers or magazines, much less television or the Net.

In 1876, eleven years after the Civil War ended, the Centennial Exposition was held in Philadelphia to celebrate the hundredth anniversary of the Declaration of Independence (Ill. 2). It was the first event

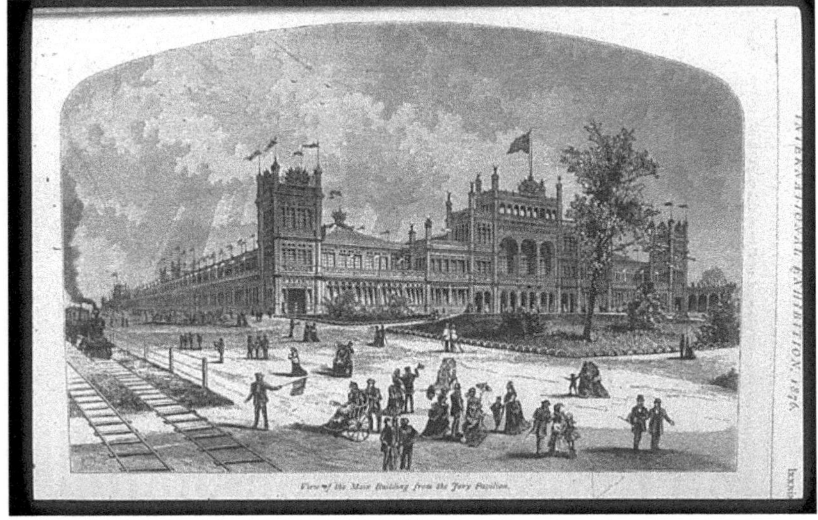

Ill. 2: Main building at the 1876 Centennial Exposition in Philadelphia.
Image: Wikipedia

in the United States that drew Americans from across the country. The Exposition was a summary of progress in science and technology. It boasted exhibitions of agriculture, education, horticulture, machinery, manufactures, and mining (Ill. 3).

Among the exhibits was the exuberant Bryant Vase, whose medallions were designed by the young Augustus Saint Gaudens (Ill. 5 and Ill. 21-23). The arm of the *Statue of Liberty* was on exhibition as part

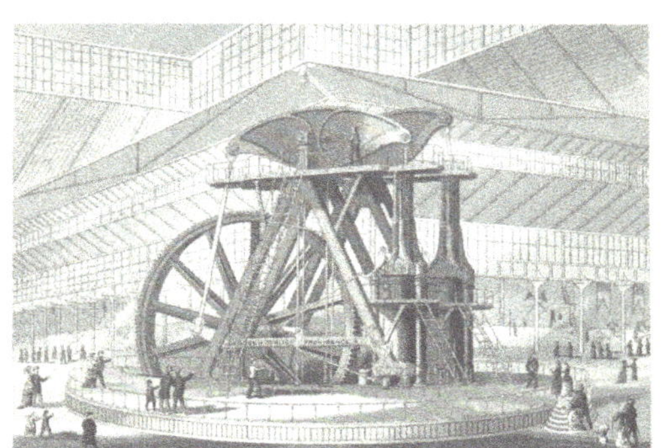
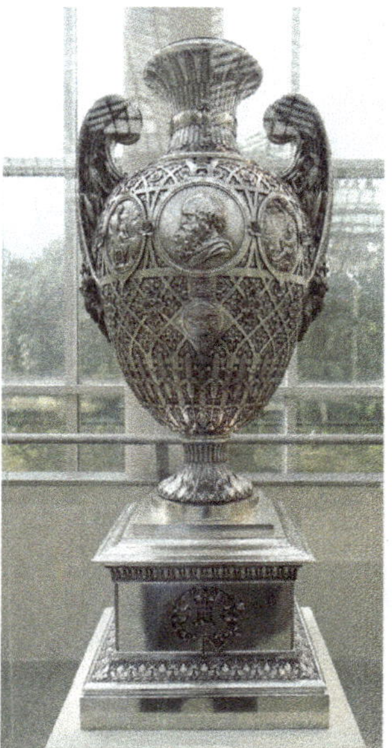
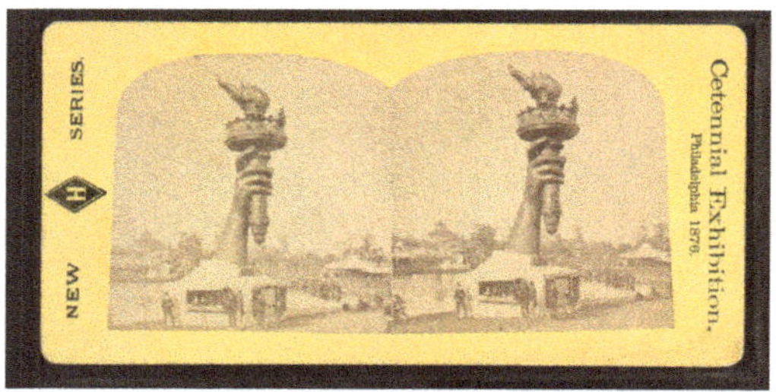

At the Centennial Exposition of 1876. Ill. 3: Corliss engine (Wikipedia). Ill. 4: arm of the Statue of Liberty (Wikipedia). Ill. 5: Bryant Vase at Metropolitan Museum of Art (Photo copyright © 2019 Dianne L. Durante)

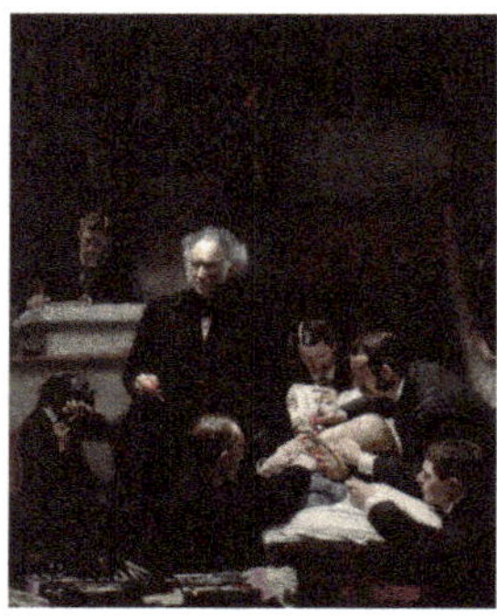
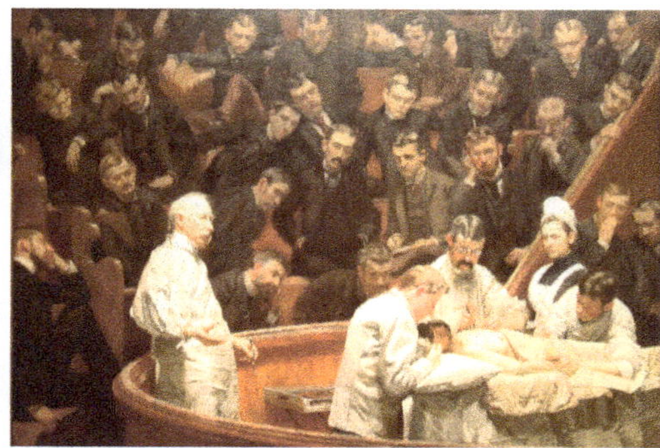

Ill. 6: Thomas Eakins, The Gross Clinic, 1875. Ill. 7: Eakins, The Agnew Clinic, 1889. Both images: Wikipedia

of a fund-raising drive (Ill. 4): the French were donating the sculpture, but the Americans had promised to raise money for its pedestal. On the whole, though, art was not the focus of the Exposition. Few artists had been trained and were working in America.

The quarter century following the Exposition was a period of tremendous progress. By 1890, only a few territories within the continental United States had not yet achieved statehood. The country's population was growing through immigration, and Americans were living longer. Life expectancy in 1800 was thirty or forty years. By 1900, it was fifty-something. That may not sound like much, but it's a 25% increase over a century earlier.

What caused that increase? In 1800, infectious disease was a leading cause of death in America. Over the course of the nineteenth century, hundreds of thousands of Americans died of cholera, typhus, yellow fever, diphtheria, dysentery, and whooping cough. By the mid-nineteenth century, clean water was being piped into cities and sewage was being channeled away from residential areas and drinking-water sources. By 1900, not one of those dread diseases was among the leading causes of death in New York City. Science, technology, and industrial progress had begun to wipe them out. Today most of us don't even recognize their symptoms.

During the 1880s, physicians began adopting asepsis—sterilizing hands and instruments and wearing scrupulously clean clothing. In two Eakins paintings of operating theaters, one from 1875 and one from 1889, the difference is startling (Ill. 6-7). Due to the adoption of asepsis, a person treated by a physician in 1900 was far less likely to die from any of the diseases that afflicted the last few patients that physician had visited.

The rate of mothers' deaths in childbirth dropped by half over the course of the nineteenth century. Infant mortality also dropped by half.

Not only was the population larger, healthier, and living longer: it was (to use a modern term) flourishing. By 1900, science and technology had dramatically increased the productivity of farmers. In 1800, 75% of Americans were farmers. By 1900, only 40% needed to be. Others could make a living with a typewriter or a sewing machine, by fixing plumbing or digging subways.

Quality of life was improving too. By 1900, many cities had electric power. Over half a million Americans had telephones. By 1910, half a million owned cars.

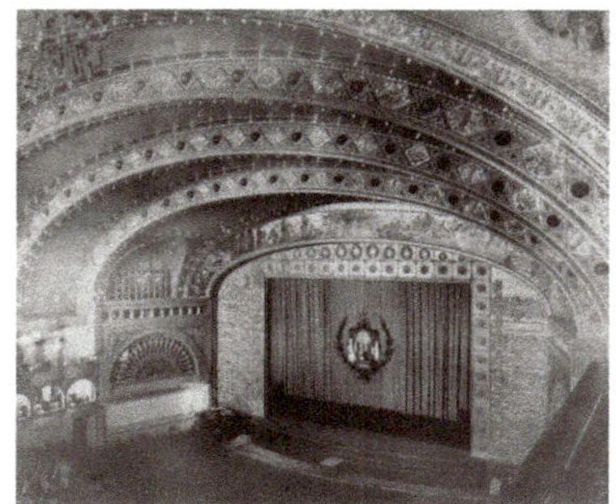
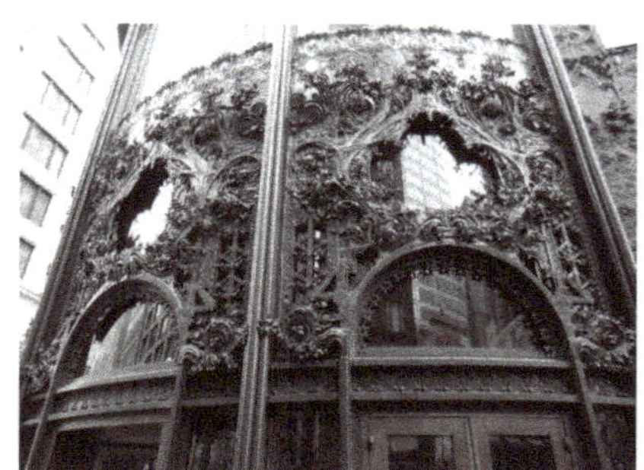
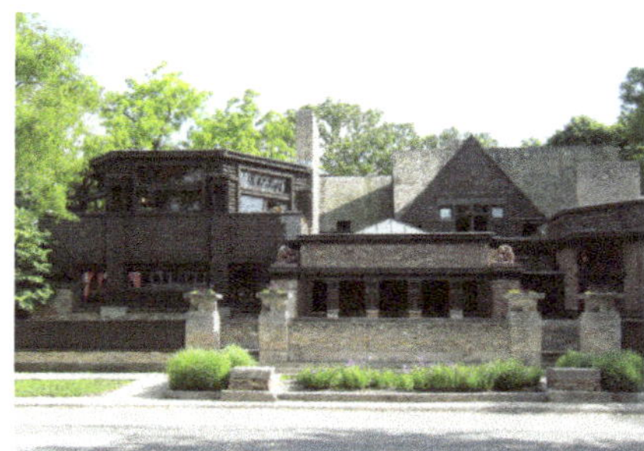
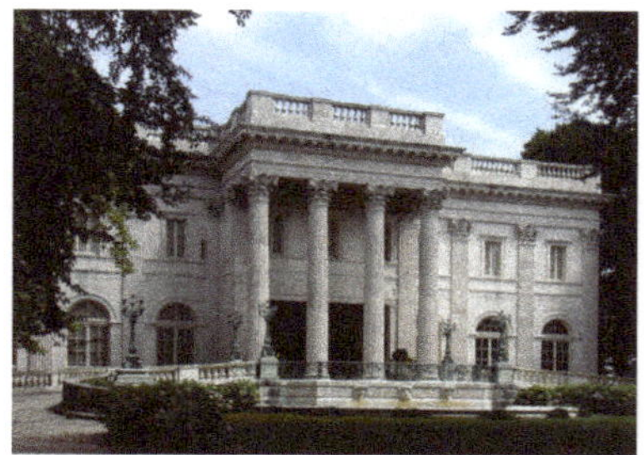
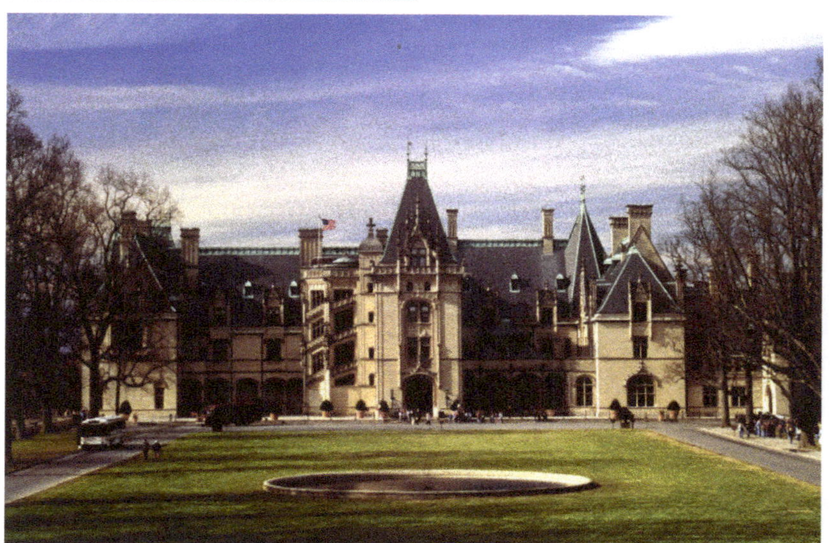

Ill. 8: Auditorium Building, Chicago, 1890. Wikipedia. Ill. 9: Carson Pirie Scott, Chicago, 1899; photo copyright © 2019 Dianne L. Durante.
Ill. 10: Frank Lloyd Wright Studio, Chicago, 1909. Zol87 / Wikipedia.
Ill. 11: Marble House, Newport, RI, 1892. Daderot / Wikipedia.
Ill. 12: Biltmore, Asheville, NC, 1895. Carptrash / Wikipedia.

Also by 1900, many Americans had money and time for "luxuries" such as art. New York City had operas, orchestras, museums, and libraries. Middle-class homes had pianos. Bachelors had player pianos. ("Wanna come hear my Chopin?")

Who was responsible for this rising standard of living? The businessmen who brought science and technology to their customers.

In 1900, the wealthiest Americans living included John D. Rockefeller (oil), Andrew Carnegie (steel), J.P. Morgan (banking), and the grandsons of Cornelius Vanderbilt (railroads). By that time, the United States was the world's leading producer of steel, coal, and oil. It was also home to many industries aimed at consumers: ready-to-wear garments, publishing, food, chemicals, drugs.

True, some reaction was beginning to stir against big business. In 1890, the first anti-trust law was passed. In 1909 came the first corporate income tax, a whopping 1%. But to most Americans, these were clouds on a distant horizon. In the last decade of the nineteenth century and the first of the twentieth, the United States came as close to capitalism as it ever did. Entrepreneurs were admired—including artist-entrepreneurs. It was expected that artists would make money if they produced a very desirable product. We'll see in the course of this book how they did that.

THE ARTS IN AMERICA CIRCA 1880-1910

What was the state of the arts in the United States at this time?

The first true skyscraper—all of twelve stories high—was erected in Chicago in 1885. In 1890, the first skyscraper taller than Trinity Church (twenty stories!) was built in New York. In 1912 the Woolworth Building topped out at sixty stories.

Many architectural styles were popular around 1900. Adler and Sullivan used elaborately beautiful decorative ornament (Ill. 8-9). Outside Chicago, Frank Lloyd Wright was creating his first Prairie Houses (Ill. 10). The homes of industrialists and other wealthy Americans might have ornament in the gothic or classical style, or have French mansard roofs (Ill. 11-12). But the period was dominated by classical architecture—and that was largely due to the Columbian Exposition.

The Columbian Exposition of 1893-1894, held in Chicago, celebrated the four hundredth anniversary of the discovery of America by Columbus (Ill. 13-15). It also celebrated the United States: its arts, culture, science, technology, and manufacturing.

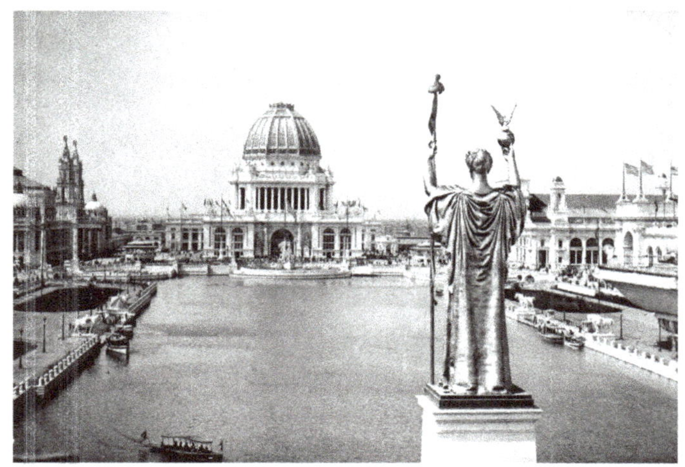

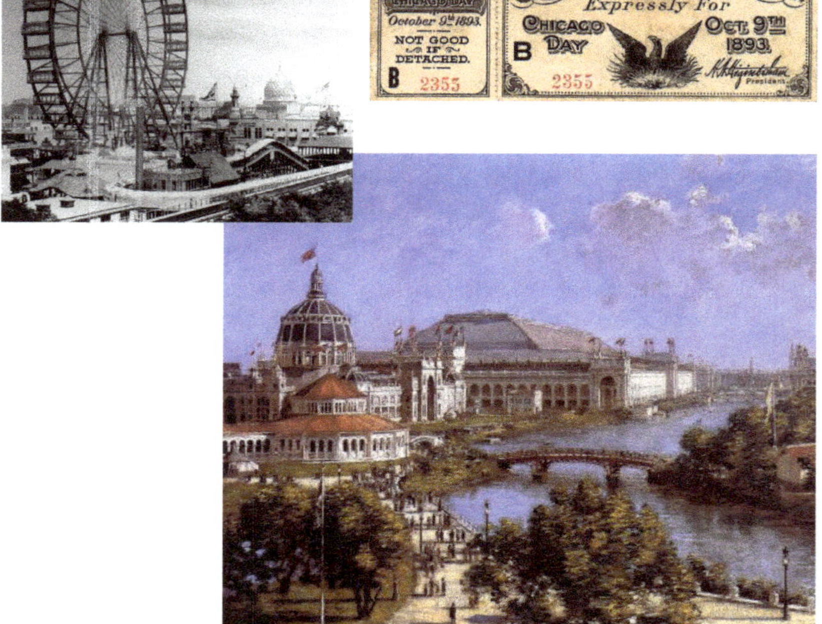

Columbian Exposition, 1893. Ill. 13: French's Republic and the Administration Building, 1893. Ill. 14A: Ferris Wheel. Ill. 14B: Ticket to Exposition. Ill. 15: Theodore Robinson, World's Columbian Exposition, 1893. All images: Wikipedia

Much of the Columbian Exposition looked forward. It offered vast displays of manufactured goods and technology. New forms of entertainment appeared, including the original Ferris Wheel, which was so large that each car held sixty people *and* a lunch counter (Ill. 14A). A whole building was devoted to women's achievements. After a fierce court battle, Sunday admission was allowed.

But the architecture of the Columbian Exposition looked back to classical models. The buildings were in the Greek and Roman style, with domes, arches, pediments, and columns. All of them were temporary, made of wood covered with plaster of Paris and hemp, then painted white to imitate marble. The fairgrounds became known as the "White City".

A year after the Exposition closed, fire ripped through the fairgrounds. Today nothing is left there. But twenty million visitors from across the country took home the memory of those shining buildings. Photos allowed millions more to view them. For the next thirty years, the "City Beautiful" movement dominated architecture. Domes, arches, columns, and pediments were the mark of state capitols, libraries, banks, railroad stations, and other important buildings across the United States (Ill. 16-17).

The centerpieces of the Columbian Exposition were sculptures in the classical style, to match its buildings. Daniel Chester French created the seventy-five-foot tall *Republic* (Ill. 13). Frederick MacMonnies created the *Ship of State* (Ill. 96-97).

We'll glance at American painting in this period when we come to Parrish. But for now, on to the eldest of our artists, Saint Gaudens.

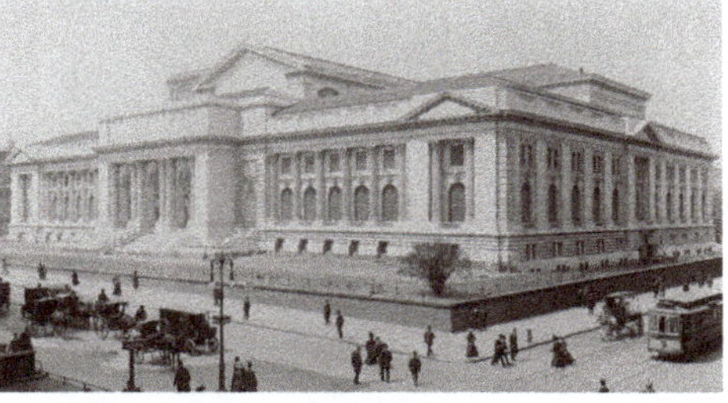

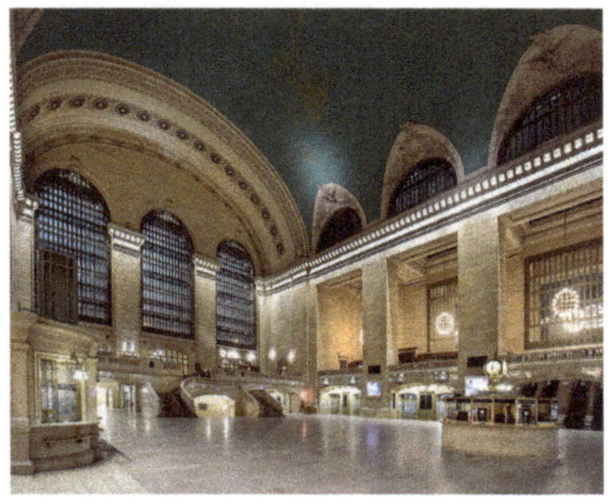

Ill. 16: New York Public Library, ca. 1908. Wikipedia.
Ill. 17: Concourse of Grand Central Terminal, New York. Metropolitan Transportation Authority of the State of New York / Wikipedia.

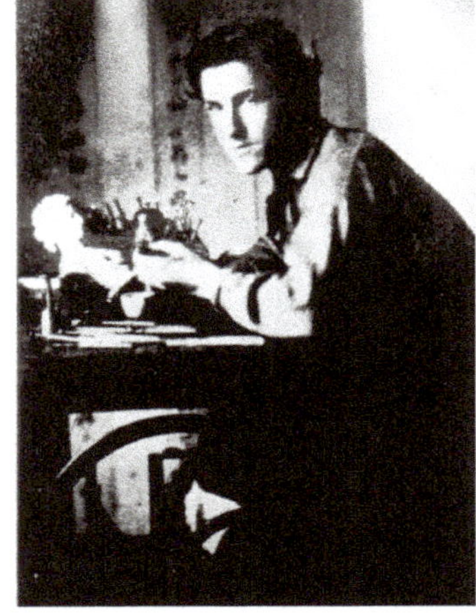

Ill. 18: Saint Gaudens at his cameo lathe, 1865. National Parks Service.

Ill. 19-20: Saint Gaudens, cameo portraits of Hannah Rohr Tuffs, 1872, and John Tuffs, ca. 1861. MetMuseum.org.

Ill. 21-23: Bryant Vase at Metropolitan Museum of Art. Photos copyright © 2019 Dianne L. Durante.

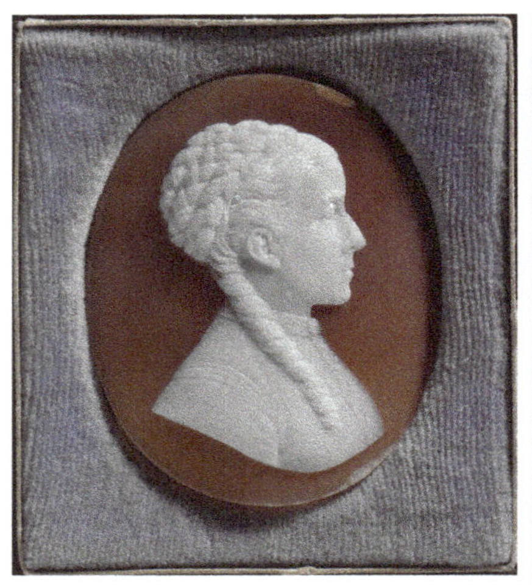

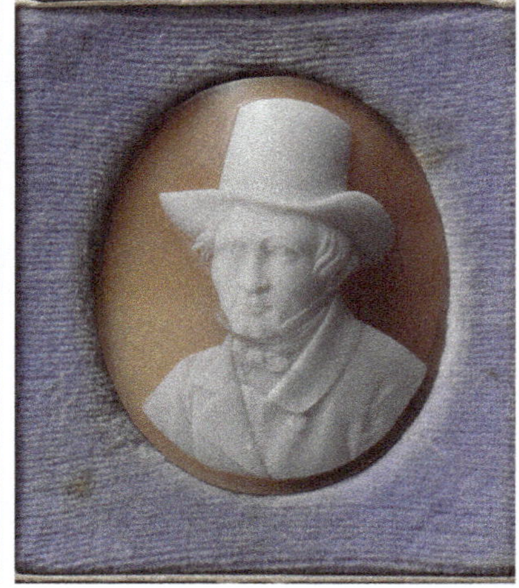

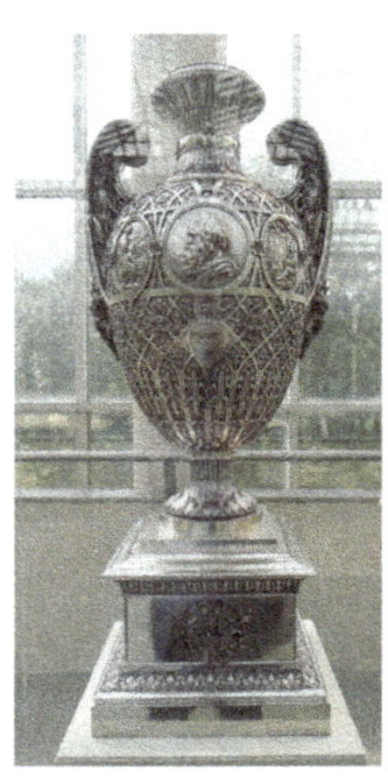

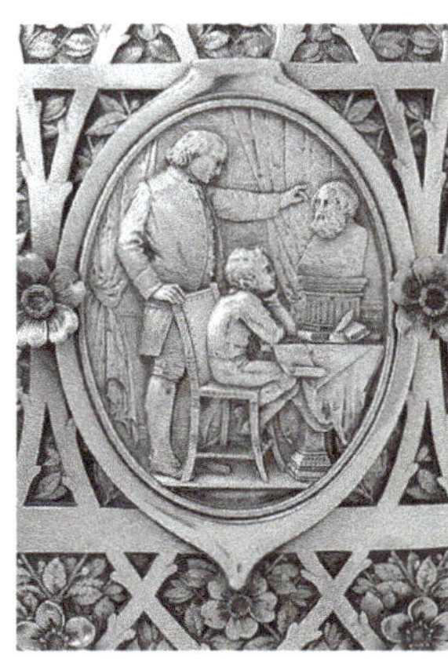

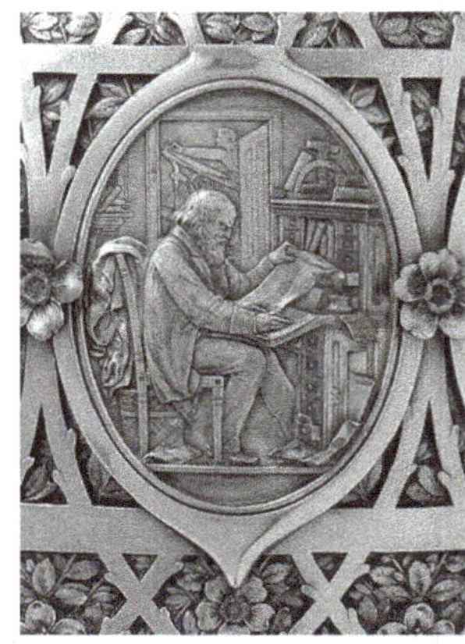

CHAPTER 2
Augustus Saint Gaudens

EARLY LIFE

Saint Gaudens was born in Dublin in 1848, the son of a bootmaker. Six months later his family immigrated to New York City. Augustus quit school at age thirteen to help support his family, spending the next three years as a cameo cutter (Ill. 18).

At his ten-hour-a-day, six-days-a-week job, Saint Gaudens learned to do exquisite portraits in low relief (Ill. 19-20). For two of those years, he also took courses at the Cooper Union: another six nights per week, several hours per night. His assignments included drawing plaster casts of ancient sculpture and drawing from live models.

In 1867, at age nineteen, Saint Gaudens scraped together enough money to study in Paris and Rome for several years. Why? Because America had very little sculpture. New York's Metropolitan Museum of Art did not open until 1872, and then with a very limited collection. To study great sculpture, one had to travel to Europe.

While Saint Gaudens was studying in Europe, he cut cameos to supplement his income. He also had a few small-scale commissions, such as the six reliefs on the Bryant Vase, which went on display at the Centennial Exhibition in Philadelphia in 1876 (Ill. 21-23; see p. 8).

As a result of long hours of study, by the 1870s Saint Gaudens had a solid knowledge of ancient and modern sculpture, of drawing, and of carving in low relief.

FARRAGUT, 1880

Saint Gaudens's big break was the *Farragut Monument* (Ill. 24, 27-29, 31). It was unveiled in 1880, when he was thirty-two. *Farragut*

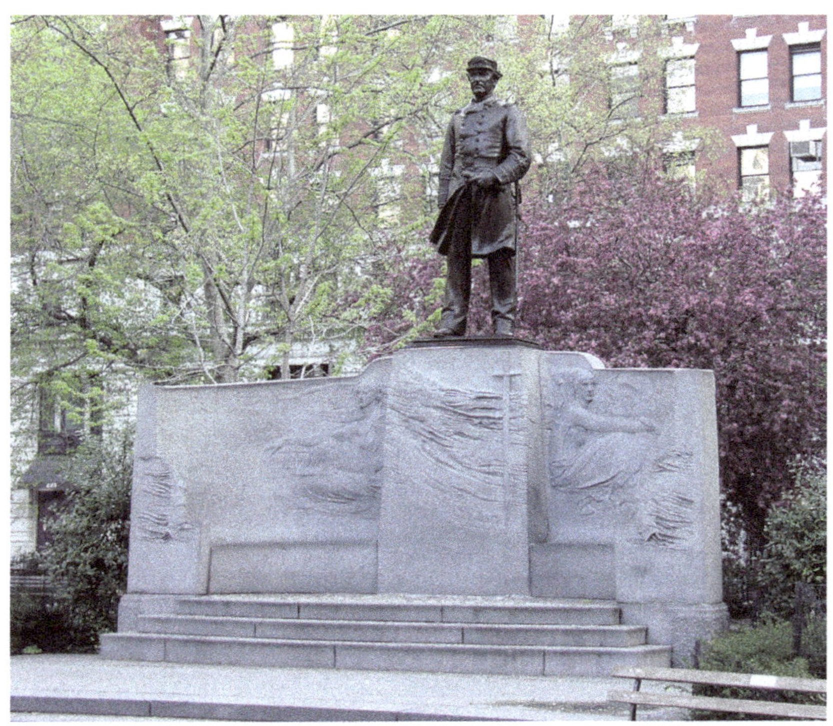

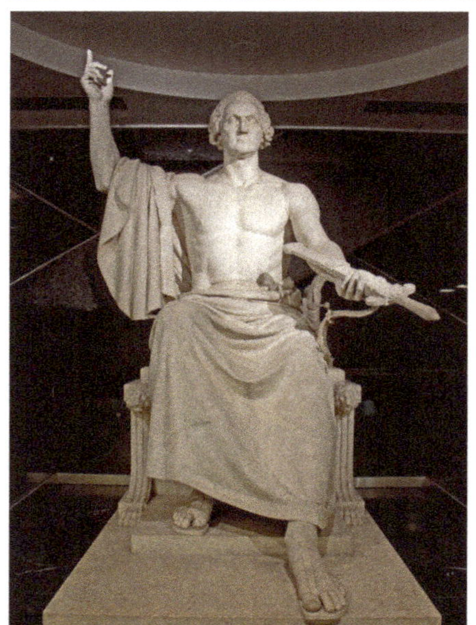

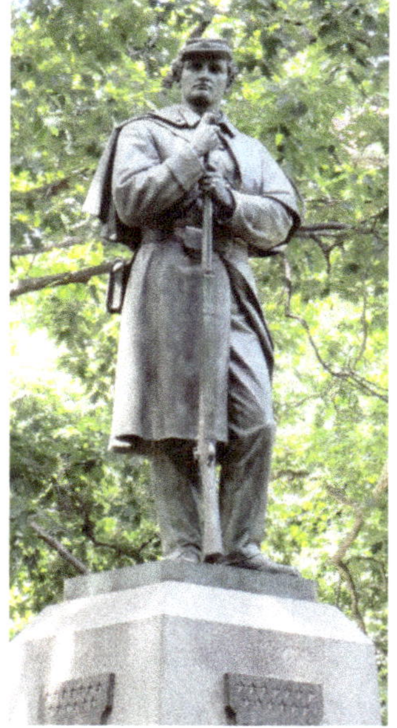

Ill. 24: Saint Gaudens, Farragut, 1880.
Ill. 25: Greenough, Washington as Jupiter, 1840. Wikipedia / Wknight94.
Ill. 26: Ward, 7th Regiment Memorial, 1869. Ill. 24 & 26:
Photos copyright © 2019 Dianne L. Durante

is a larger-than-life-size bronze figure on a pedestal fifteen feet wide and seven feet high. The monument stands in New York's Madison Square, at Fifth Avenue and Twenty-Sixth Street.

First of all: who is David Glasgow Farragut? Answer: a hero. He was the most celebrated naval commander of the Civil War, which had ended fifteen years before this work was dedicated. Farragut captured New Orleans and won the Battle of Mobile Bay. At Mobile Bay, he had himself lashed to the rigging so he could see the course of the fighting. When one of his ships hit an underwater mine (also known as a torpedo), he shouted to his men, "Damn the torpedoes! Full speed ahead!"

Farragut is a man on a wall, and at first sight, he's not very exciting. We need to understand what made this sculpture such a great success, or the rest of Saint Gaudens's career will be incomprehensible. So let's step back for a moment and look at the context: the type of portrait sculptures normal at this time.

The first common style of sculpture was Neoclassical, imitating Greek and Roman works. Hence we have representations of the Founding Fathers in classical garb (Ill. 25).

The second common style is illustrated in the works of John Quincy Adams Ward, America's leading sculptor by 1880, when *Farragut* was dedicated. Among many others, Ward had created *Indian Hunter,* the *Seventh Regiment Memorial* (Ill. 26), and *Shakespeare* (Ill. 32), all of which stand in Central Park. As opposed to the Neoclassicists, Ward stressed that Americans should look like Americans. His portrait sculptures have great physical likenesses and beautifully executed details.

When the *Farragut* commission came up, every American sculptor wanted it. It was given to Ward, but he had many other commissions at the time, so he recommended Saint Gaudens, who was eighteen years his junior.

Saint Gaudens introduced several innovations in *Farragut*. First of all, *Farragut* is standing as if on the deck of his flagship, guiding his men, looking for the enemy. How do we know? Because he's holding binoculars, and his coat is blowing open (Ill. 27). *Farragut* wears a U.S. Navy uniform, meticulously represented (Ill. 27-28, 30).

In short: *Farragut* is shown going about his business. The figure reveals his character and actions. It reminds us why he's honored with a sculpture. Think of the difference between doing a portrait of me with my hands demurely folded, or one with my hands gesturing and pointing, which they usually are. Saint Gaudens has shown not just a

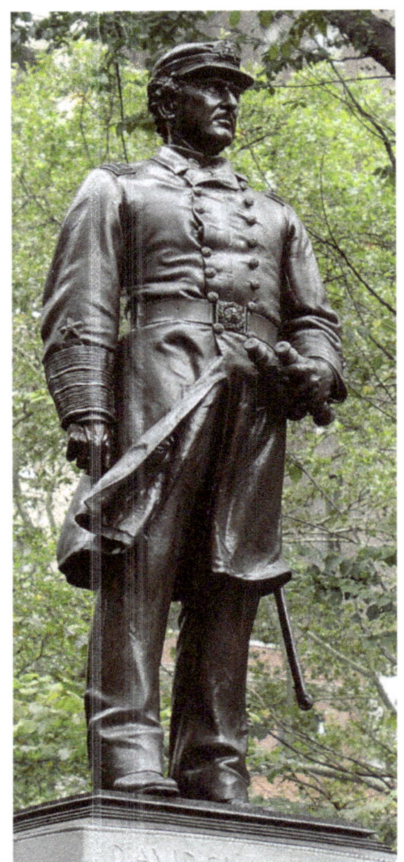

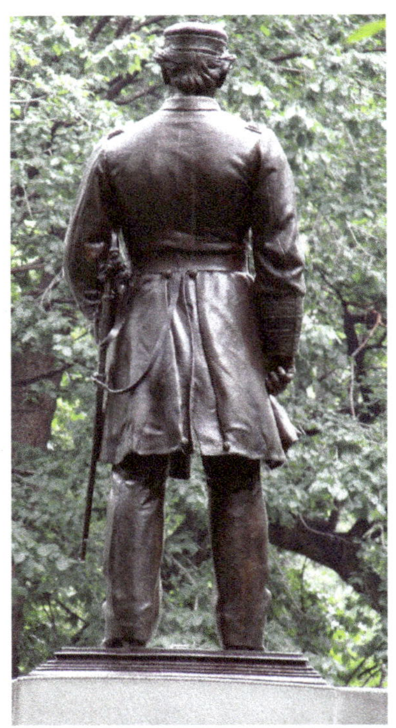

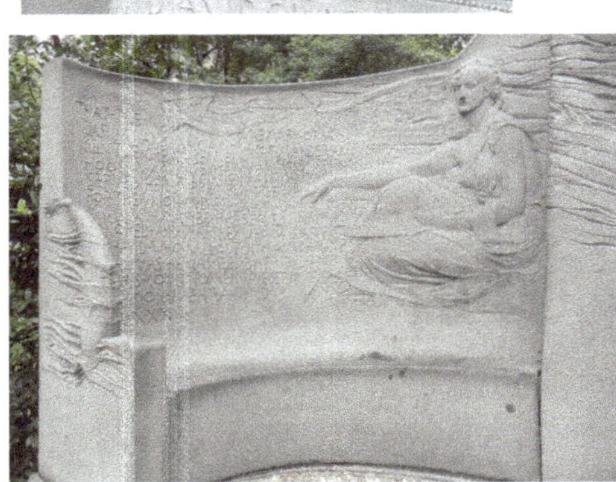

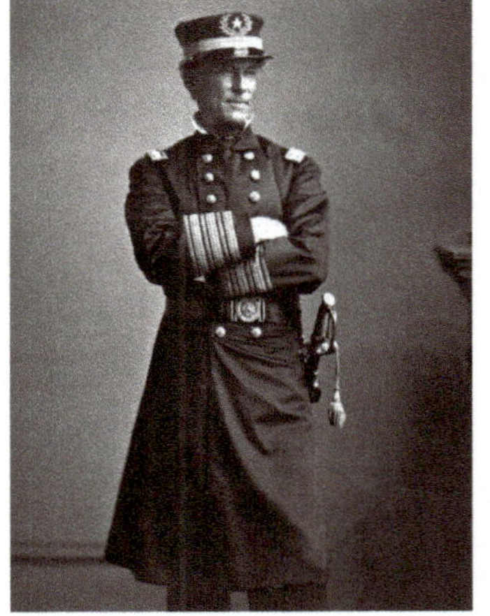

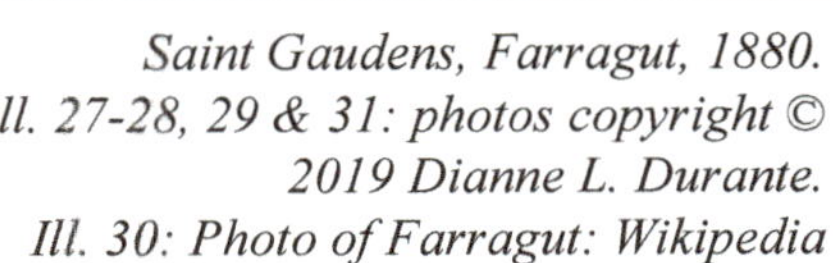

Saint Gaudens, Farragut, 1880.
ll. 27-28, 29 & 31: photos copyright ©
2019 Dianne L. Durante.
Ill. 30: Photo of Farragut: Wikipedia

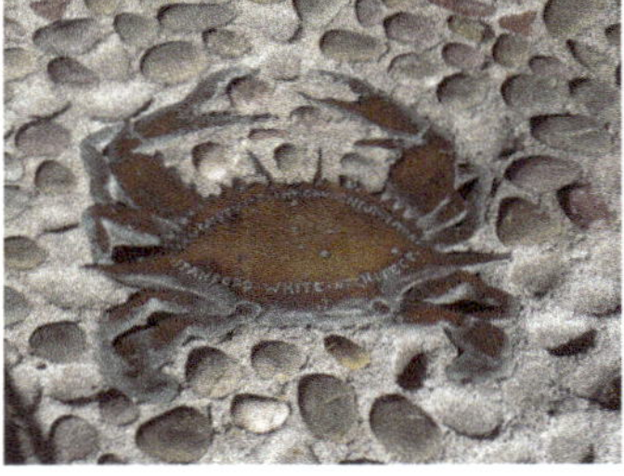

physical resemblance, but something about the character of the man. That's why *Farragut* was so striking to contemporaries. This is true of all Saint Gaudens's portraits, as we'll see.

But that's not the only innovation in *Farragut*. The usual pedestal for a portrait sculpture was an all-purpose rectangle, suitable for anyone (Ill. 32). Saint Gaudens collaborated with architect Stanford White on the *Farragut* pedestal, creating an ensemble around a heroic figure. The pedestal is curved: we have to go close to see all of it (Ill. 24). On either side is a lengthy inscription about his service to his country (Ill. 29). We don't need to read the inscription to identify the figure as a heroic naval officer, but if we do, it adds something to our knowledge of him. The sword and waves on the pedestal show that he's a military man at sea (Ill. 24).

Saint Gaudens liked to combine allegorical and real figures to convey more than a portrait alone could. The reliefs on the base are of Loyalty and Courage (Ill. 29). They remind the viewer that Farragut was brave and loyal to his country.

Incidentally, this pedestal is a harsh copy on granite done by Works Progress Administration artists. By the 1930s, the original marble pedestal had been severely damaged by automobile exhaust fumes— something Saint Gaudens couldn't have predicted when he created the work. The original base is now at the Saint Gaudens National Historical Park in Cornish, New Hampshire.

If we come right up to the steps of *Farragut*'s pedestal, we're rewarded with a delightful detail. On the pebbled ground at the base of the pedestal, the sculptor's and architect's signatures are inscribed on a bronze crab (Ill. 31).

So: *Farragut* is an accurate portrait. The figure's stance and costume, plus the motifs on the pedestal, show his character and actions. This combination of figure plus pedestal is suitable for a monument to David Glasgow Farragut—and no one else.

Saint Gaudens worked on *Farragut* for four years. He did model after model of

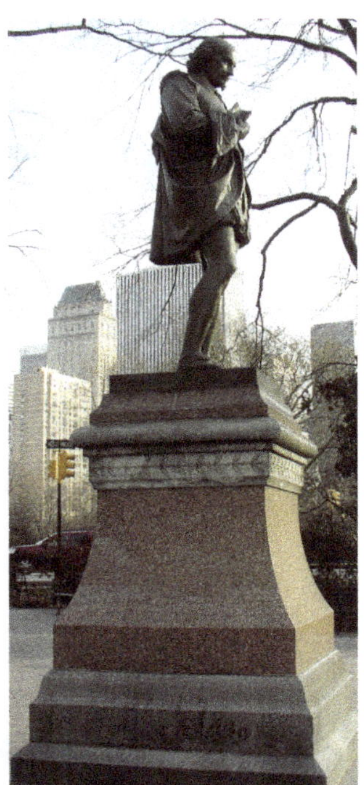

Ill. 32: Ward, Shakespeare, 1872. Photo copyright © 2019 Dianne L. Durante

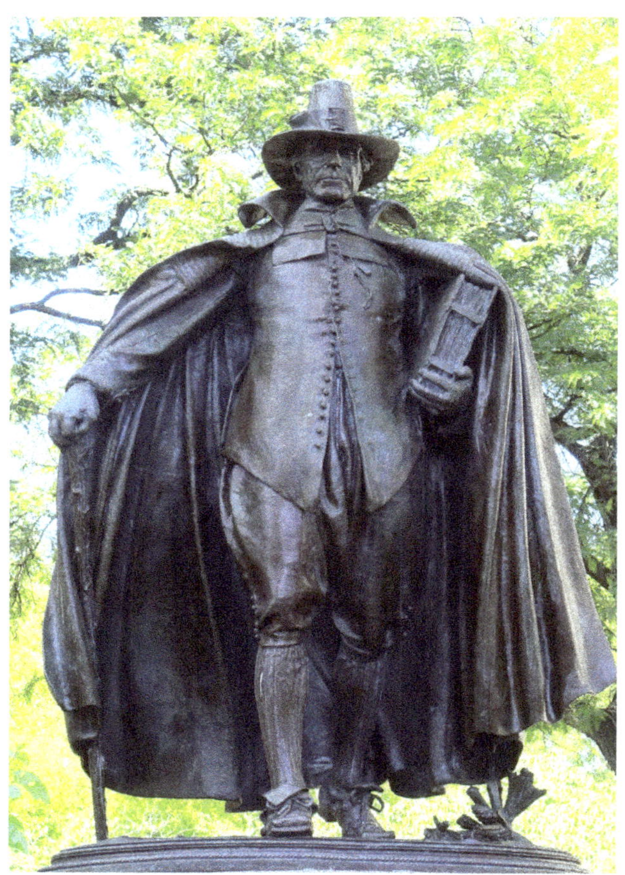

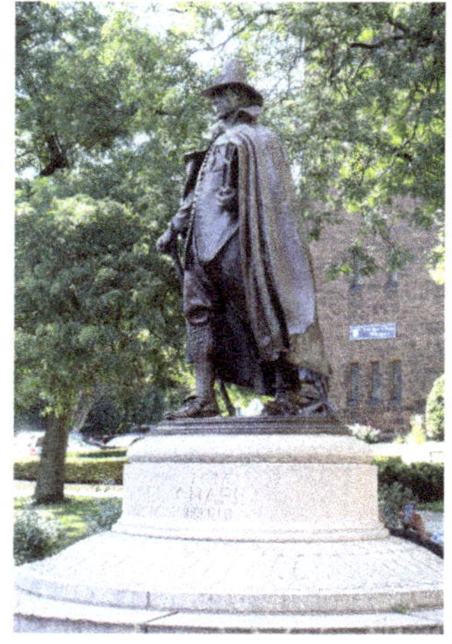

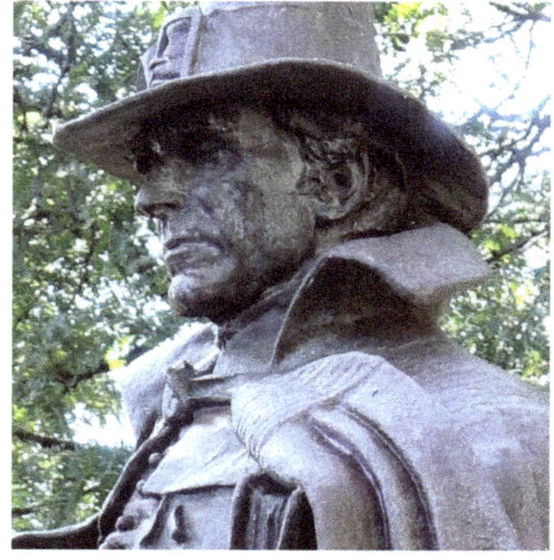

Ill. 33-35: Saint Gaudens, Puritan, 1887. Springfield, MA.
All photos: Daderot / Wikipedia

various parts. He reworked the lettering. He supervised it from clay model to plaster cast to bronze.

In 1879, a year before the dedication, he wrote to a friend:

> All my brain can conceive of now is arms with braid, legs, coats, eagles, caps, legs, arms, hands, caps, eagles, eagles, caps and so on; nothing, nothing but that statue. —Quoted by Thayer Tolles in "Augustus Saint-Gaudens in The Metropolitan Museum of Art," *MMA Bulletin*, Spring 2009

We've spent all this time on *Farragut* because this level of innovation and this much attention to detail and execution are characteristic of Saint Gaudens's work at the beginning of his career and throughout his life.

PURITAN, 1887

The *Puritan* was commissioned to honor Deacon Samuel Chapin, a seventeenth-century founder of Springfield, Massachusetts (Ill. 33-35). It looks like our standard image of a Pilgrim or Puritan, right? But … there was no standard image in Saint Gaudens's time. Saint Gaudens had the Chapin family research seventeenth-century wood-cuts to learn what the clothing should be. Then, said Saint Gaudens, "I developed it into an embodiment, such as it is, of the 'Puritan'" (quoted on the Metropolitan Museum's page for the *Puritan*).

Sometimes it's difficult to appreciate Saint Gaudens's works because they seem so typical. But in many cases, it was Saint Gaudens who created the image we think of as typical.

I've written about this sculpture at length in three posts on DianneDuranteWriter.com. The first of the three is at https://diannedurantewriter.com/archives/4299.

LINCOLN, 1887

The next sculpture (Ill. 43-47) is another example of Saint Gaudens creating our standard image. *Lincoln* was a different sort of challenge from the *Puritan*. In the 1870s and 1880s, tens of thousands of people still remembered Lincoln—how he looked and how he moved. And of course thousands of photos were in circulation (for example, Ill. 36-38).

Sculptors began creating portrait statues very soon after Lincoln was assassinated. New York's *Lincolns* by Henry Kirke Brown, in Prospect Park and Union Square, date to 1868 and 1869 (Ill. 39-42).

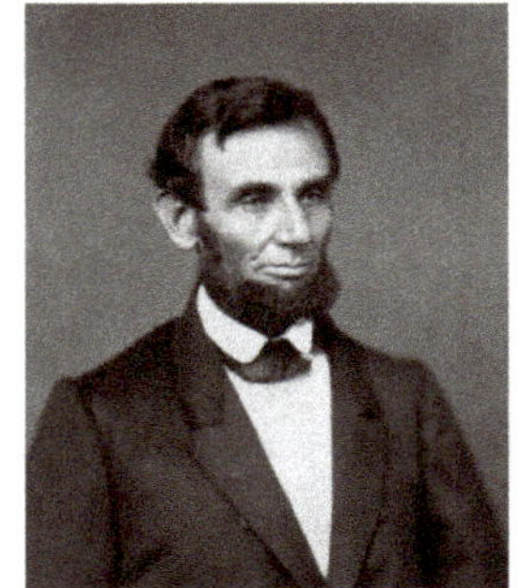
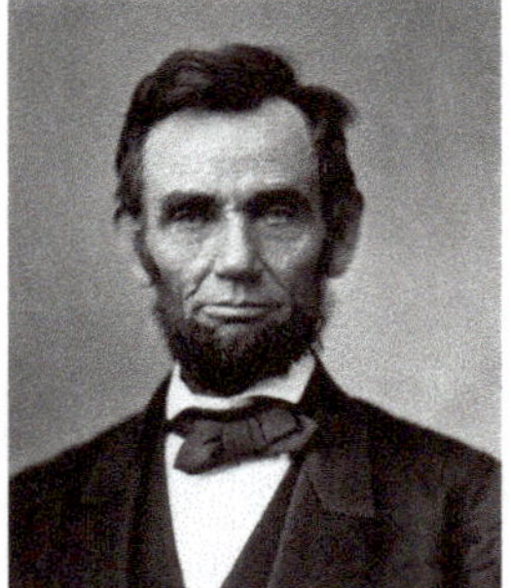
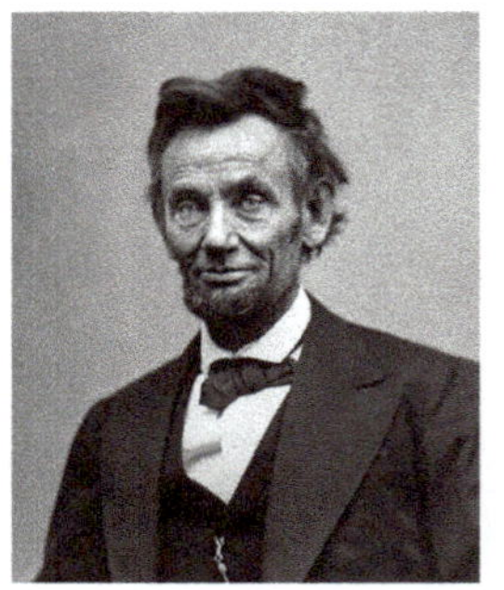
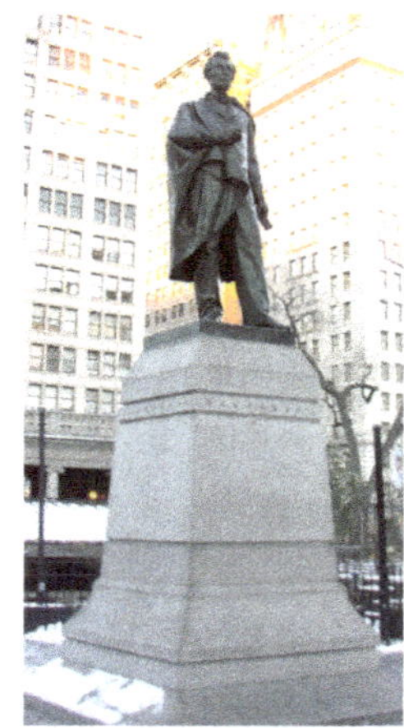
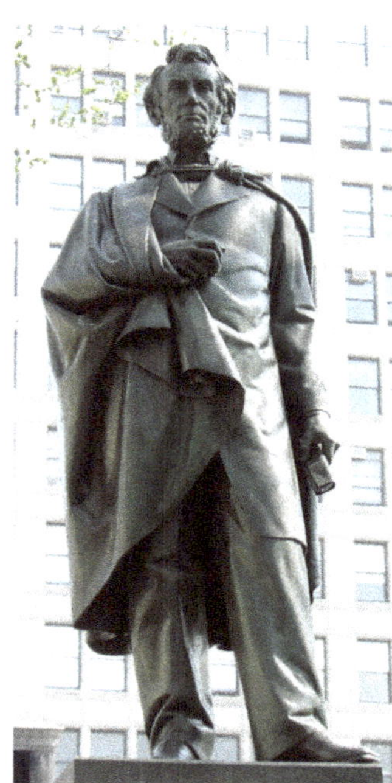
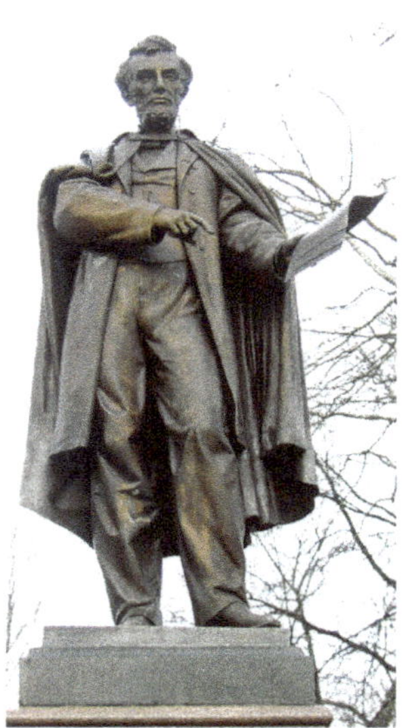
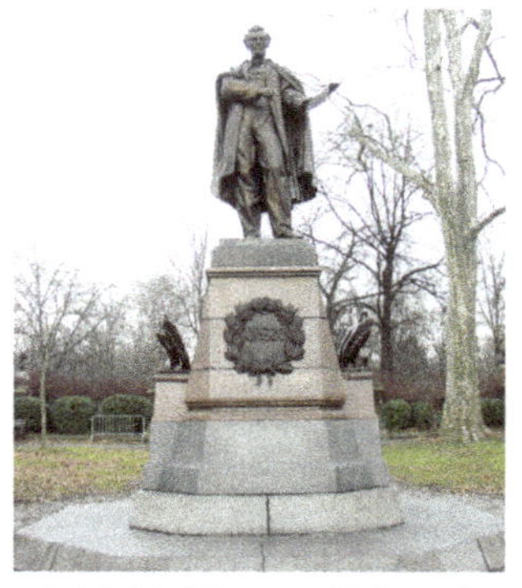

Ill. 36-38: Lincoln in 1861, 1863, and 1865. Photos: Wikipedia
Ill. 39-40: Brown, Lincoln, 1868. Union Square, New York.
Ill. 41-42: Brown, Lincoln, 1869. Prospect Park, Brooklyn.
Ill. 39-42 Photos copyright © 2019 Dianne L. Durante

They're typical of early sculptures of Lincoln. Each wears a voluminous cape, similar to a toga—a nod to Neoclassicism, which was the accepted way to make leaders of the time look dignified and important (cf. Ill. 25). The faces look like Lincoln's, but there's no distinctive character to the bodies. They would suit a politician, a soldier, a writer, or an industrial tycoon.

Saint Gaudens was commissioned to create a sculpture of Lincoln for Chicago. As a teenager he had seen Lincoln in a parade, and he had also seen him lying in state in New York City in 1865. Saint Gaudens acquired casts of Lincoln's hands and face. He studied photos. He read Lincoln's writings and speeches. He even moved his studio to Cornish, New Hampshire, in part because someone told him the state had "Lincoln-sized men". (The heat of New York City summers before air conditioning was also a factor in the move.)

Saint Gaudens's home base was New York, so he had certainly seen Brown's *Lincolns,* and probably other sculptures of Lincoln as well. He proceeded to break the mold.

Saint Gaudens created an accurate physical portrait of Lincoln, but he also shows the man at a characteristic moment: head bowed, hand holding his lapel (Ill. 43-44). One leg is forward, but the weight is on the back leg, so he can't be moving forward. He seems to have paused for thought. This *Lincoln* wears contemporary American clothes that

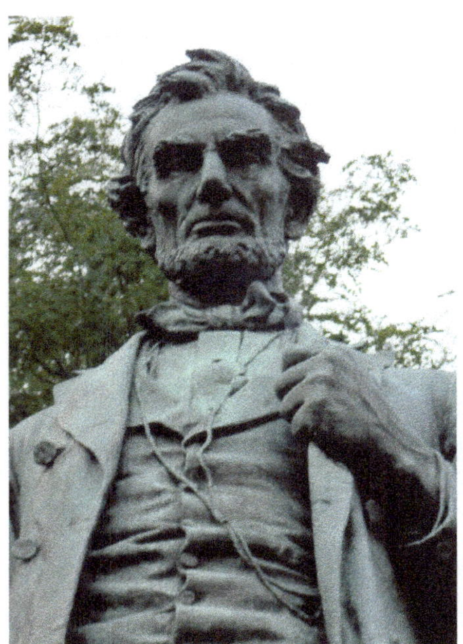
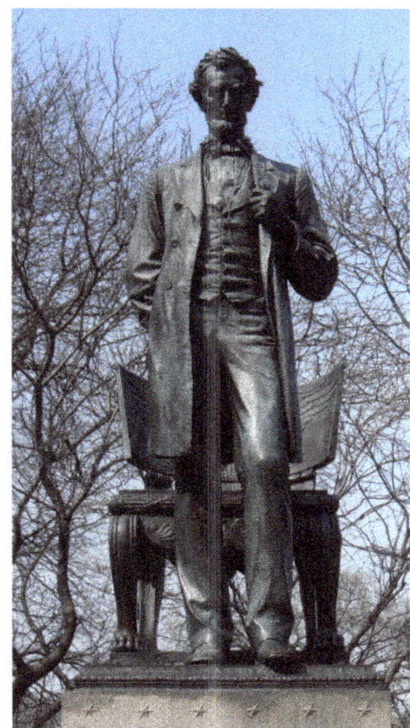

Ill. 43-44: Saint Gaudens, Lincoln, 1887.
Photos: Johnym1_2 and Zagalejo_2 / Wikipedia

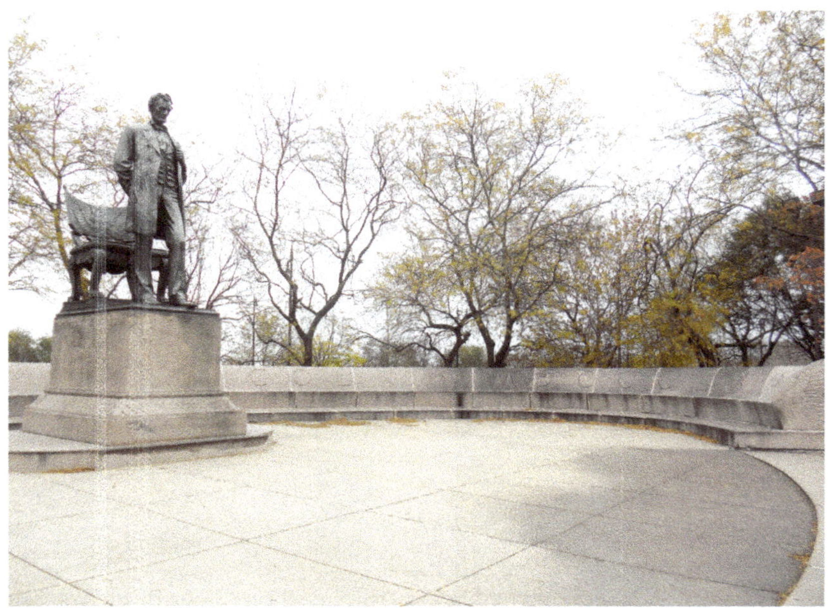

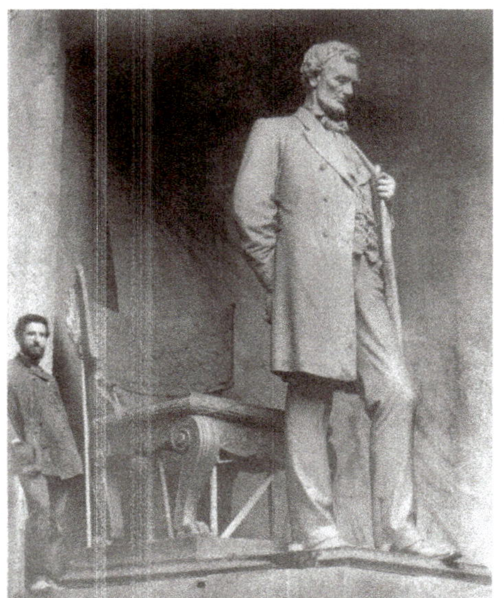

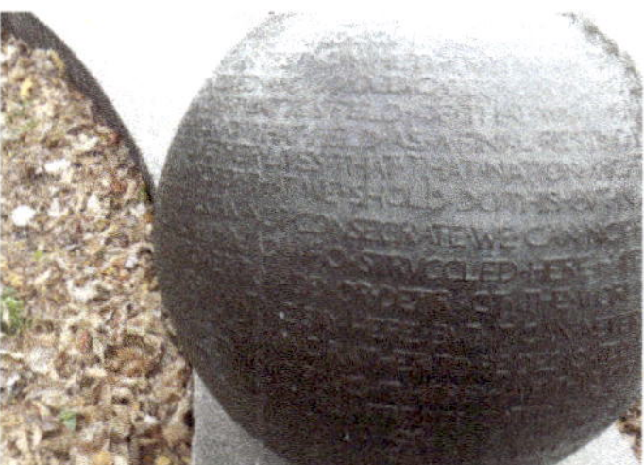

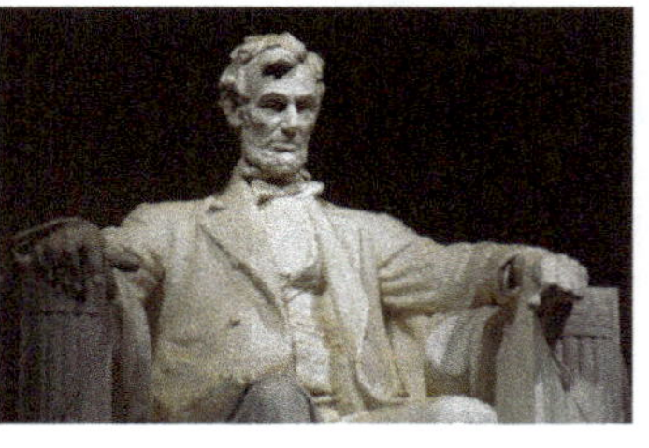

Ill. 45-47: Saint Gaudens, Lincoln, 1887; the figure at left in Ill. 46 is Saint Gaudens. Ill. 45, 47: Photo copyright © 2019 Dianne L. Durante. Ill. 46: National Parks Service. Ill. 48A: Daniel Chester French, Lincoln from the Lincoln Memorial, 1920. Photo: Jeff Kubina / Wikipedia.

have somehow been made to look timeless. As opposed to the *Lincolns* by Henry Kirke Brown, Saint Gaudens's figure is gaunt. The effect: this *Lincoln* is a strong, austere thinker, a leader of men and of a nation at war. He's also a literal giant, twelve feet high (Ill. 46).

For this figure, Saint Gaudens designed another ensemble. Behind the figure is a chair with an eagle on the back, suitable only for a president. The plaza in which the figure and the chair stand is sixty feet in diameter (Ill. 45). The *Lincoln* in Union Square has been crowded in by trees and food vendors and playgrounds. The *Lincoln* in Chicago can't be overshadowed by such distractions. The plaza has a bench and a wall at the back edge, so we can't approach except from the front, and by climbing the steps. He's literally someone to look up to.

At either end of the steps are two spheres bearing excerpts from Lincoln's most famous speeches (Ill. 47). Two more quotes are inscribed on the back of the wall. None of these quotes are large or distracting, but they let us know more about Lincoln and remind us why he's worth commemorating.

Saint Gaudens's contemporaries agreed that this was the finest portrait sculpture ever created in the United States. It has become our standard image of Lincoln. The only other sculpture that's even close to this iconic is Daniel Chester French's *Lincoln* in the Lincoln Memorial (Ill. 48A). That one was done forty years later, and it incorporates the austere, brooding mood of Saint Gaudens's.

STEVENSON, 1887 OR LATER

Saint Gaudens's bas-relief of Robert Louis Stevenson (1850-1894; Ill. 48B) was begun in 1887, the same year *Lincoln* was dedicated in Chicago. When Saint Gaudens did sketches for it, Stevenson was already ill. He died seven or eight years later of tuberculosis or sarcoidosis … or one of those other deadly nineteenth-century diseases. But instead of showing a thirty-seven-year-old who was seriously ill and skeletally thin, Saint Gaudens showed a man reading papers as he relaxed against pillows, a cigarette in one hand.

Profile reliefs had been done in Roman times and the Renaissance, but no one had ever done a portrait relief that revealed quite this much character. Although the relief is less than half an inch deep, it suggests three-dimensional space. The figure is remarkable for the way it fits the frame and the way the inscription fits around it. All those years of cameo-cutting paid off with reliefs such as this.

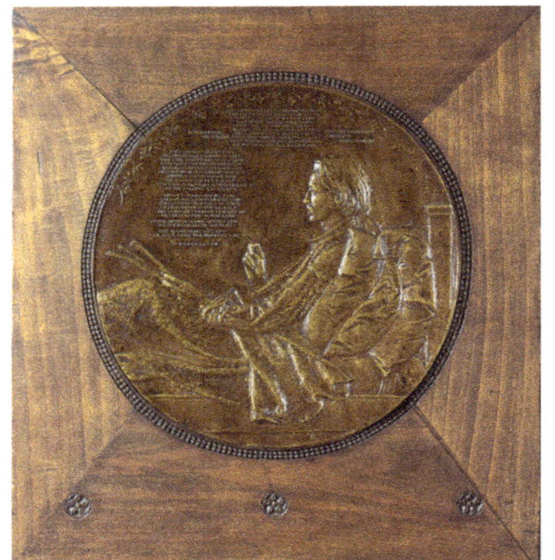
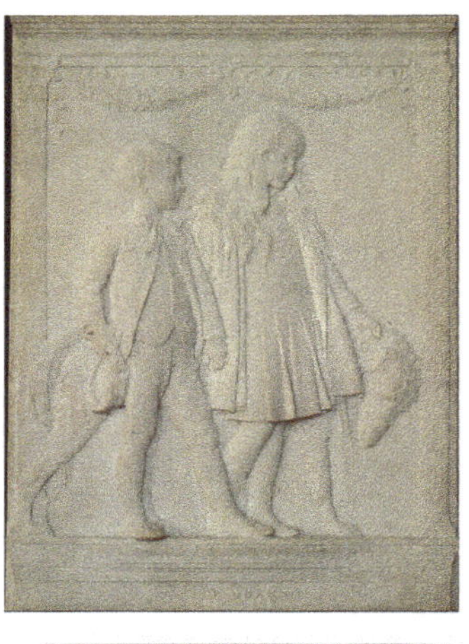
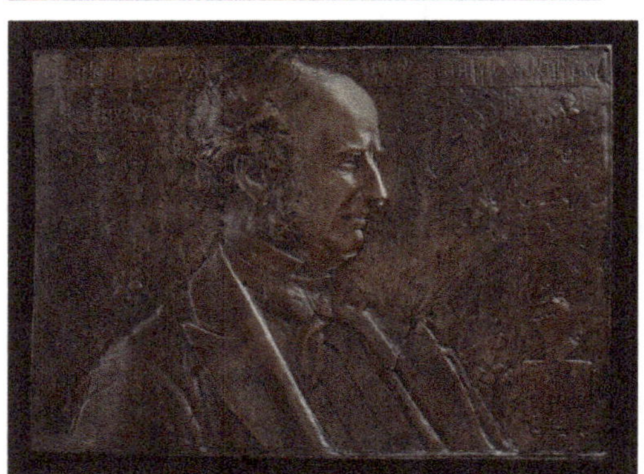
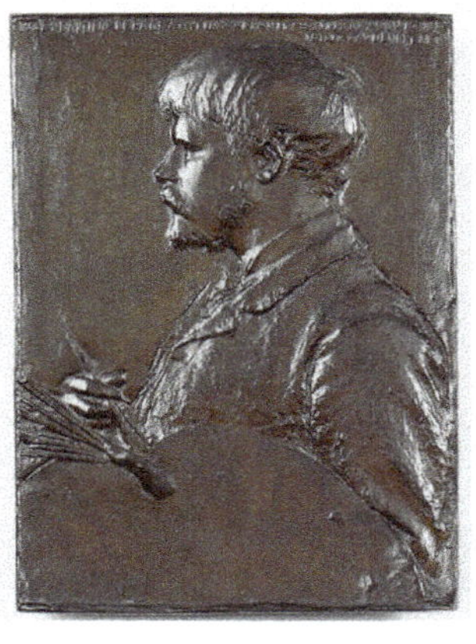
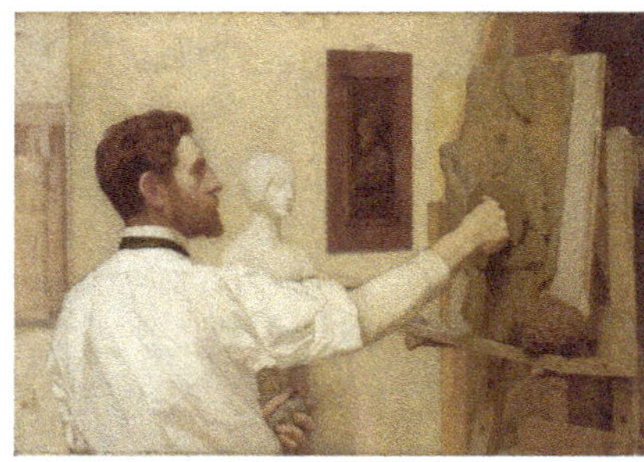
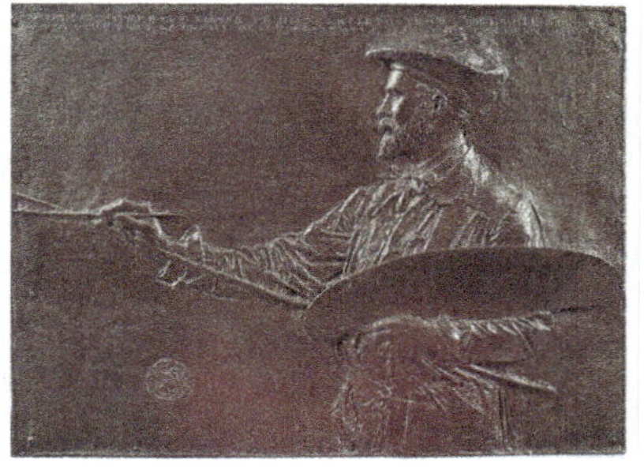

*Bas reliefs by Saint Gaudens. Ill. 48B: Robert Louis Stevenson, 1887-1888.
Ill. 49: Schiff Children, 1884-85. Ill. 50: Cornelius Vanderbilt, 1882.
Ill. 51: Jules Bastien LePage, 1880. Ill. 52: Kenyon Cox, Augustus Saint
Gaudens, 1908 copy of 1887 original. Ill. 53: William Merritt Chase, 1888;
American Academy of Arts and Letters. All others: MetMuseum.org*

Over his thirty-year career, Saint Gaudens did thirty-five major monuments such as *Lincoln* and *Farragut*. He also did more than eighty bas-relief portraits such as *Stevenson*, and every single one of them is worth looking at (Ill. 49-51 and 53). My favorite among these is of painter William Merritt Chase, in which Saint Gaudens made the left edge of the relief function as the "canvas" that Chase is painting (Ill. 53). In Kenyon Cox's painted portrait of Saint Gaudens, this is the relief Saint Gaudens is working on (Ill. 52).

Such reliefs were not on the same grand scale as Saint Gaudens's monumental works, but because they were small and portable, they helped spread his reputation.

ADAMS MEMORIAL, 1891

The *Adams Memorial* looks simple, but it took three years to complete (Ill. 54-55). Saint Gaudens smashed at least three models and started again from scratch. The seated figure has been interpreted as hope, serenity, atheism, and despair. Creating something so simple and so unforgettable is no easy task. And it shows that Saint Gaudens's range is wider than one might think, looking only at *Farragut, Lincoln,* and the *Puritan.*

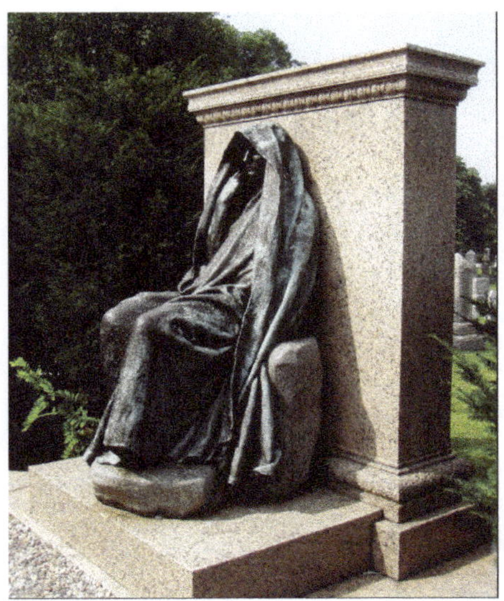
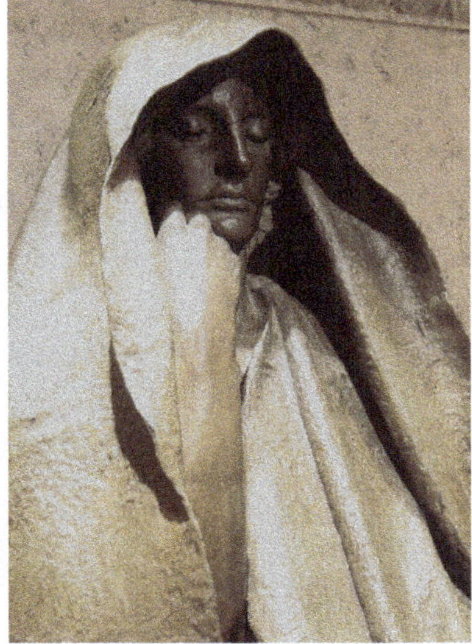

Ill. 54-55: Saint Gaudens, Adams Memorial, 1891.
Danvera_2 and red_herring / Wikipedia

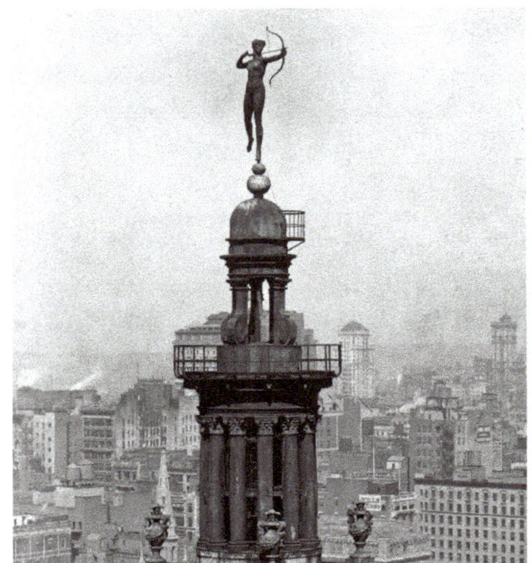

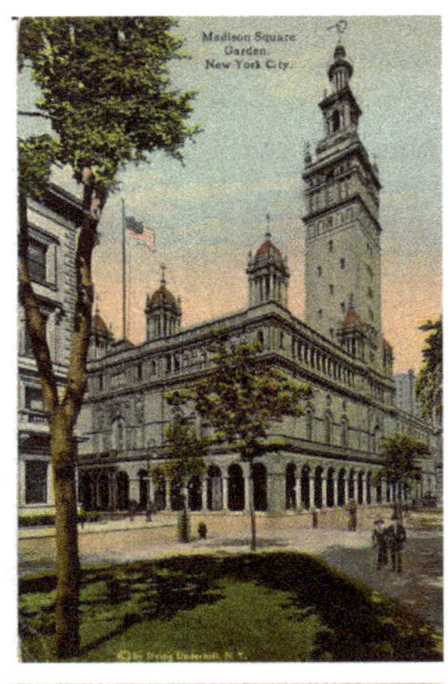

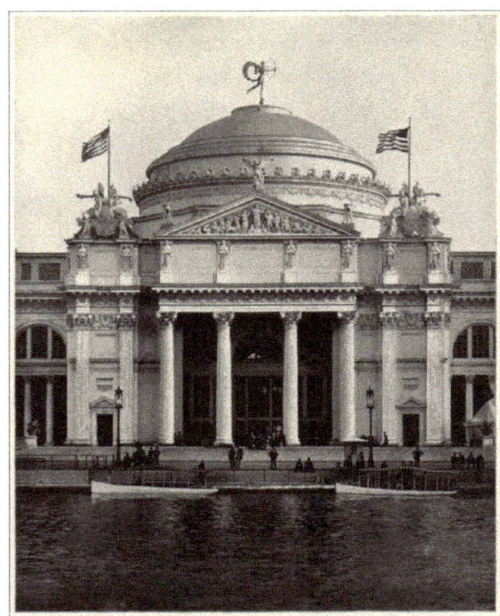

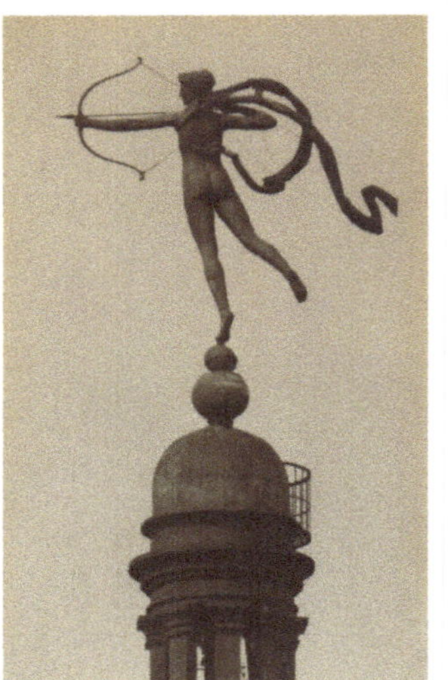

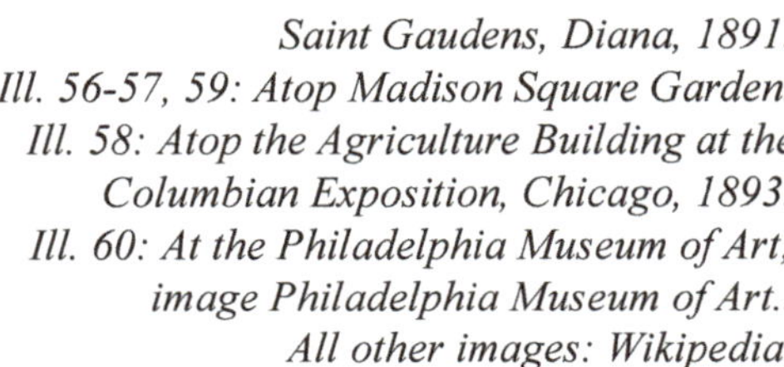

Saint Gaudens, Diana, 1891.
Ill. 56-57, 59: Atop Madison Square Garden.
Ill. 58: Atop the Agriculture Building at the
Columbian Exposition, Chicago, 1893.
Ill. 60: At the Philadelphia Museum of Art;
image Philadelphia Museum of Art..
All other images: Wikipedia.

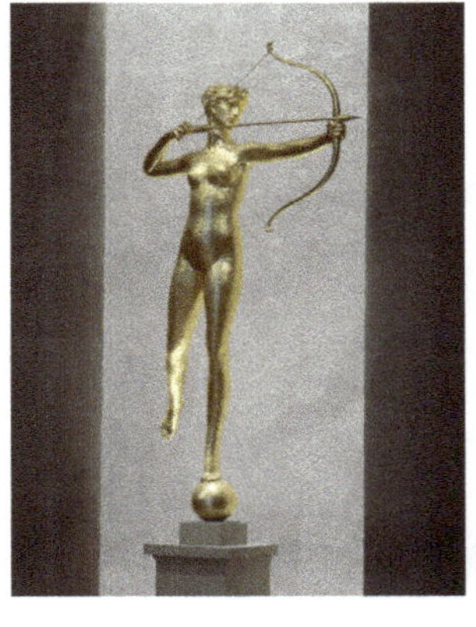

DIANA, 1891

Diana was set in place the same year as the *Adams Memorial* was dedicated. This gilt figure of a naked woman balances on one leg and draws a bow. She stood atop the second Madison Square Garden, an all-purpose pleasure palace at Madison Avenue and Twenty-Third Street (Ill. 56-57). *Diana* was poised forty-two feet higher than the *Statue of Liberty*—higher than the tallest Manhattan building. She was the first thing in Manhattan that the sun touched in the morning, and the last thing it touched at night. She was also the first outdoor sculpture in New York to be illuminated at night by electricity, and the first sculpture of a naked woman to be prominently placed outdoors in Manhattan. A few mothers reportedly covered the eyes of their children when passing by, but most New Yorkers loved the sculpture.

It's difficult to imagine *Diana* any other way, but in the original version she flaunted a single curl of drapery (Ill. 59). *Diana* was designed as a weathervane, and the curl of drapery helped her spin.

Saint Gaudens and architect Stanford White soon decided the original version was too large for the building. They removed it temporarily to one of the buildings at the Columbian Exposition in Chicago (Ill. 58). The fire that ripped through the fairgrounds also destroyed the sculpture. On Madison Square Garden, a smaller *Diana*—thirteen feet rather than eighteen—was erected. That one eventually ended up in the Philadelphia Museum of Art (Ill. 60).

SAINT GAUDENS AS ENTREPRENEUR

By 1891—eleven years after the dedication of the *Farragut*—Saint Gaudens's major commissions included *Farragut, Puritan, Lincoln,* the *Adams Memorial,* and *Diana.* He was in great demand for such works, and was paid well for them. But such commissions took years to complete, and expenses were difficult to predict.

Saint Gaudens found a new way to bring in regular income: he made smaller copies of his major works for sale to the general public. In the 1890s, one could walk into Tiffany's and purchase a three-foot-tall bronze reproduction of the *Puritan* or *Diana* (Ill. 61-64). Some of these still come up for sale occasionally, for tens of thousands of dollars.

Another way in which Saint Gaudens made money was to take more commissions and delegate more of the routine work. In the early 1890s, he had studios for different projects at Twentieth,

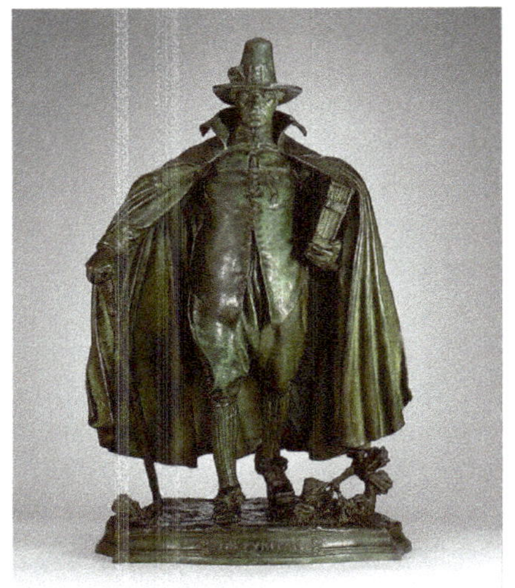

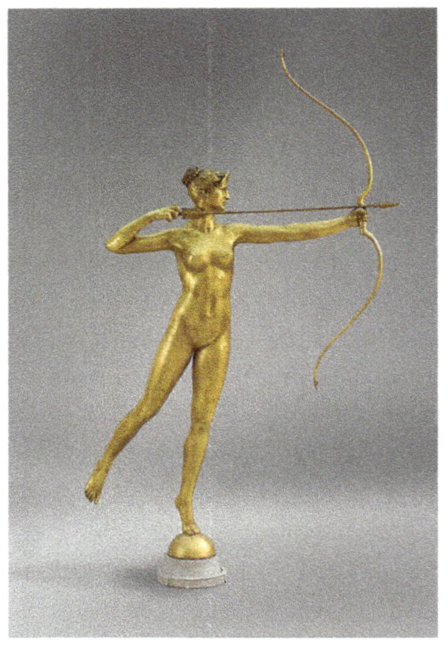

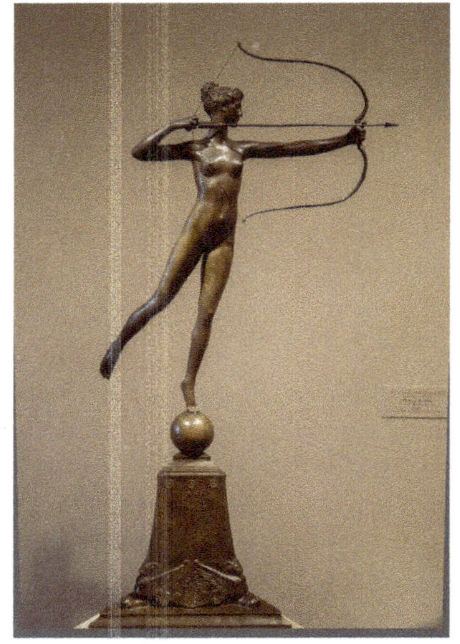

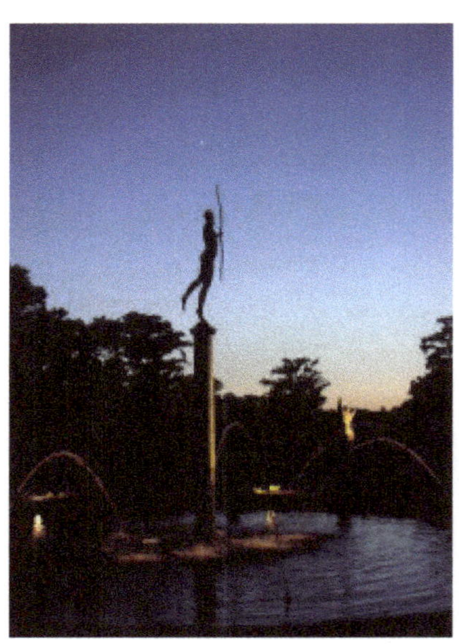

Saint Gaudens reductions. Ill. 61: Puritan. MetMuseum.org.
Ill. 62: Diana. MetMuseum.org
Ill. 63: Diana. Wikipedia.
Ill. 64: Diana at Brookgreen Gardens.
Photo copyright © 2019 Dianne L. Durante

Twenty-Seventh, Thirty-Sixth, and Fifty-Ninth Streets in Manhattan. But Saint Gaudens always designed every piece, supervised the work of his assistants at every stage (e.g., building the armatures and shaping the most basic forms), and applied the finishing touches.

SHAW MEMORIAL, 1897

The *Shaw Memorial,* on Boston Common, honors Col. Robert Gould Shaw, leader of the first regiment of black soldiers during the Civil War (Ill. 65). He died with many of his men in an attack on Charleston. (The movie *Glory* is based on Shaw's life.)

It took Saint Gaudens two years to get this commission and thirteen years to complete the memorial. Here's his explanation of why he spent so much time on his sculptures.

> A sculptor's work endures for so long that it is next to a crime for him to neglect to do everything that lies in his power to execute a result that will not be a disgrace …. It is plastered up before the world to stick and stick for centuries, while men & nations pass away. —Quoted in *Reminiscences of Augustus Saint-Gaudens,* ed. Homer Saint-Gaudens (New York: Century, 1913; repr. New York: Garland, 1976)

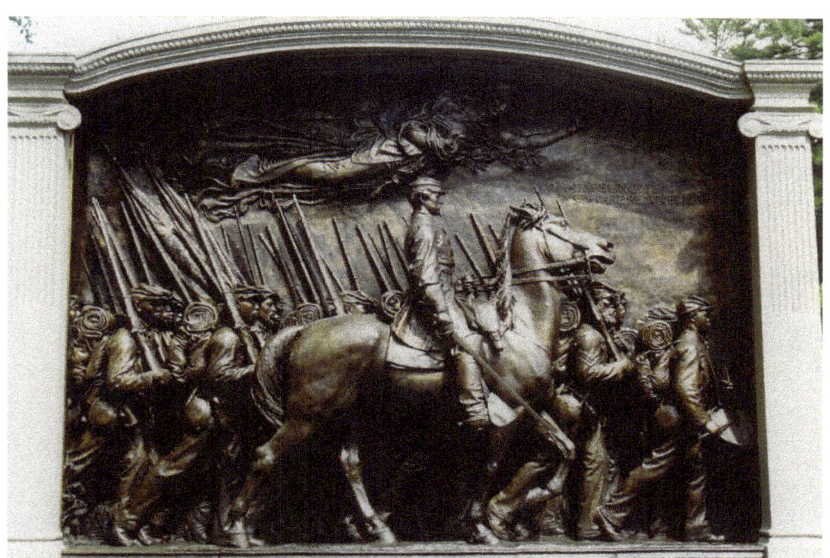

Ill. 65: Saint Gaudens, Shaw Memorial, 1897. Boston Common.
Photo: Carptrash / Wikipedia

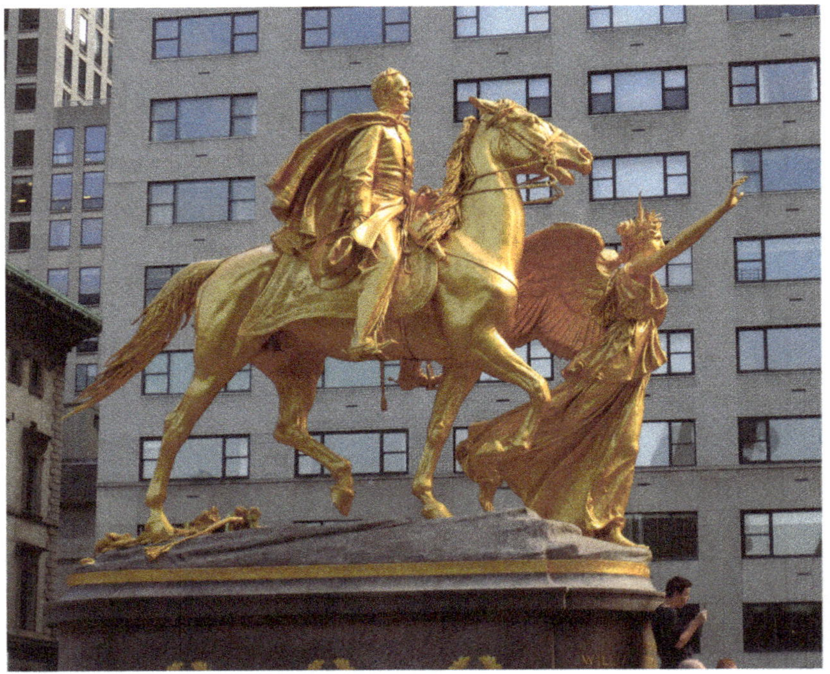

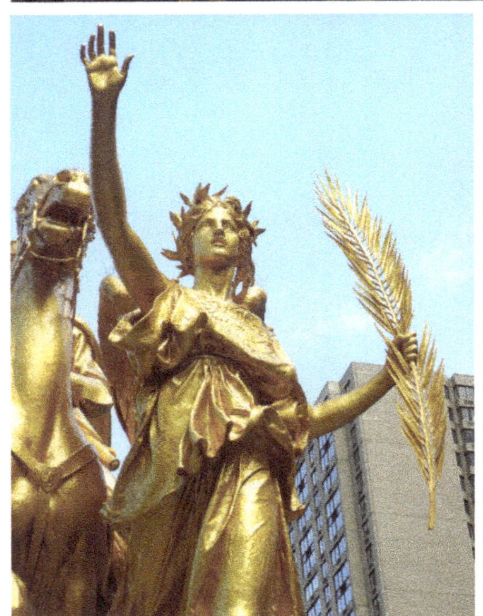

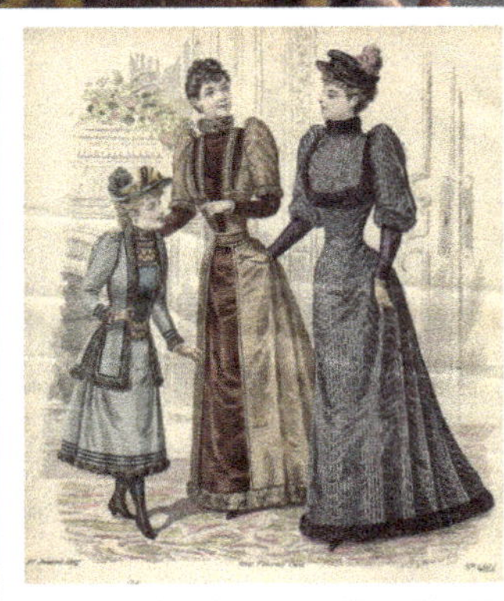

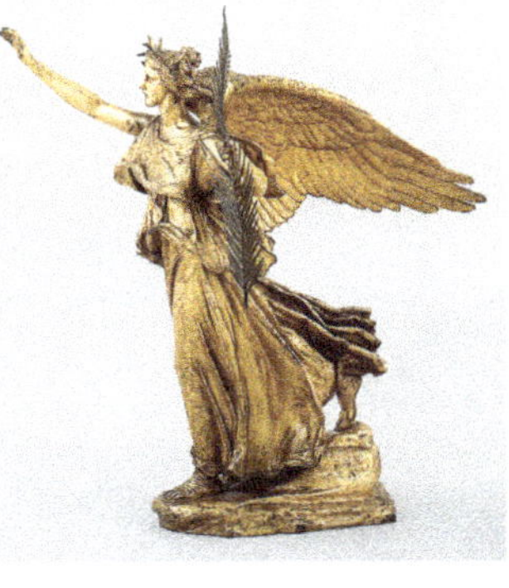

Saint Gaudens, Sherman, 1903.
Ill. 66-67: Photos copyright © 2019
Dianne L. Durante
Ill. 68: Godey's Lady's Book / Wikipedia.
Ill. 69: MetMuseum.org

SHERMAN MONUMENT, 1903

Saint Gaudens's memorial to William Tecumseh Sherman stands at the southeast corner of Central Park (Ill. 66-67). Sherman is best known (some would say notorious) for his march through Georgia, which cut Confederate supply lines and demoralized the Deep South, thus hastening the end of the Civil War. Americans honored him for that: they even proposed him as a presidential candidate. He told them, "If nominated, I shall not run. If elected, I shall not serve." It was said he never acknowledged an error, and never repeated one. Incidentally, his brother was Senator John Sherman, who sponsored the Sherman Anti-Trust Act.

What's notable about this sculpture? First, Sherman is presented as a hero: there's no ambiguity. The face is very accurate, because Saint Gaudens based it on a portrait bust he had sculpted of Sherman in 1888. Like *Farragut's*, the uniform here is rigorously accurate. *Sherman*'s upright military posture is emphasized by cape billowing behind him, which gives him swagger. Take the cape away, and he'd seem less heroic and less energetic.

Sherman's horse is led by an allegorical figure of Victory (Ill. 67, 69). On her head is a laurel wreath, symbolizing victory. In her hand is a palm branch, symbolizing peace. Victory is unusual among female figures at this time. In the 1890s the ideal woman was petite, wore a stiff corset and voluminous petticoats, and minced about (Ill. 68). Victory is not Victorian: she's tall, athletic, and confident, yet very feminine.

It's not easy to combine a real figure with an allegorical one. Saint Gaudens has done it not just by having Victory lead *Sherman's* horse, but by repeating the vertical and slanted lines in the two figures (Ill. 70).

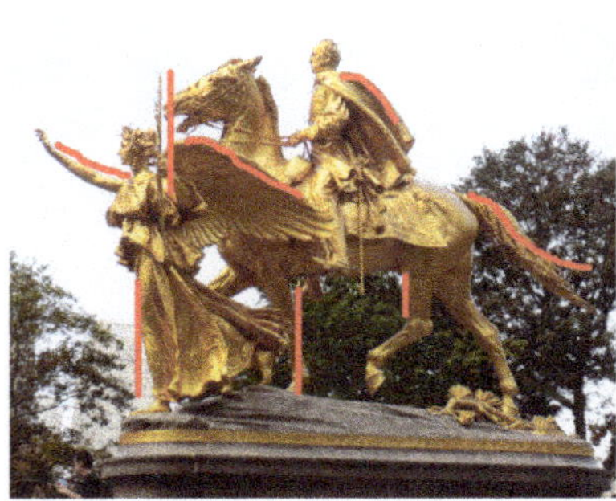
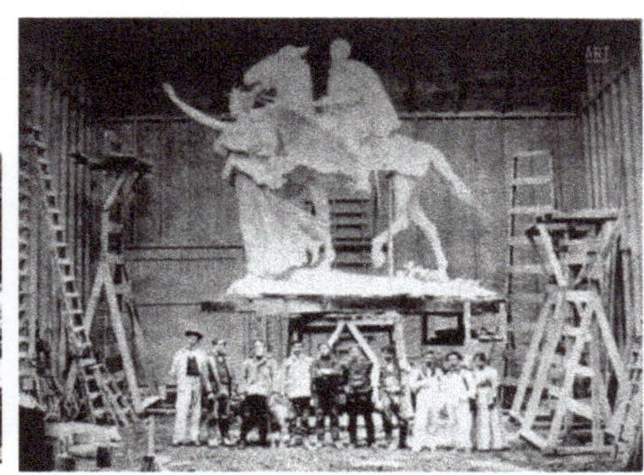

Ill. 70: Saint Gaudens, Sherman, 1903.
Photo copyright © 2019 Dianne L. Durante.
Ill. 71: Saint Gaudens with assistants and Sherman.
Photo via DaytonianinManhattan.blogspot.com

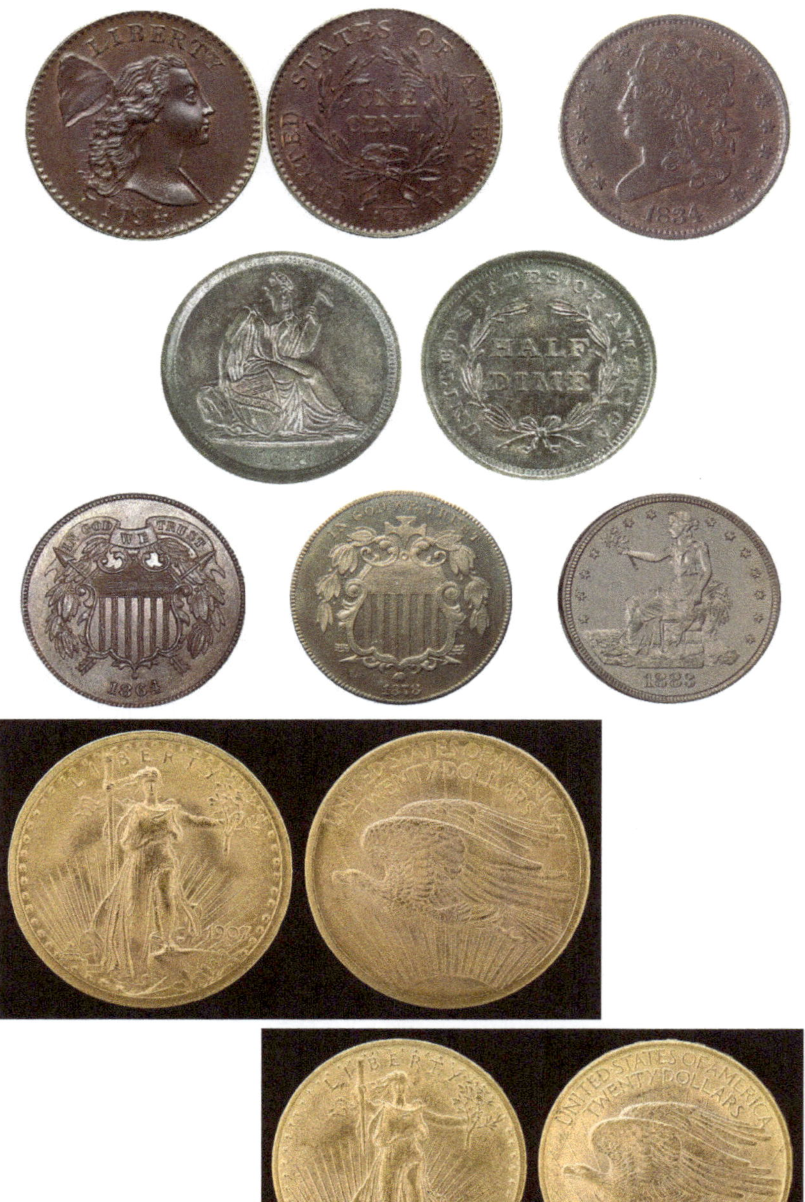

United States coins. Ill. 72-73: 1794. Ill.74: 1834. Ill. 75-76: 1837.
Ill. 77: 1864. Ill. 78: 1873. Ill. 79: 1883.
Ill. 80: Saint Gaudens "Walking Liberty" double eagle as issued in 1907.
Ill. 81: "Walking Liberty" as issued in 1908. All images: Wikipedia

Sherman was Saint Gaudens's last major monument. Although he had been ill for a decade, he meticulously planned every detail, including the type of gold used for the surface and the angle at which the sculpture should be positioned to catch the light. For a perfectionist such as Saint Gaudens, making such decisions might require more time than executing them. His son Homer recalled his father trying to impress this attitude on his assistants (shown with him in Ill. 71).

> "I am going to invent a machine to make you all good sculptors..."
> The stillness promptly became uneasy.
> "It will have hooks for the back of your necks, and strong springs."
> The stillness grew even more uneasy.
> "Every 30-seconds it will jerk you fifty feet away from your work, and hold you there for five minutes' contemplation." — Quoted in *Reminiscences of Augustus Saint-Gaudens*, ed. Homer Saint-Gaudens (New York: Century, 1913; repr. New York: Garland, 1976), I, 293

COINS

We'll look at one last work by Saint Gaudens: the Walking Liberty gold coin. American coinage had been designed since Alexander Hamilton's time by employees of the U.S. Mint. President Theodore Roosevelt considered it to be in a state of "artistically atrocious hideousness" (Ills. 72-79). In 1905 he invited Saint Gaudens, America's pre-eminent sculptor, to redesign several coins. Saint Gaudens lived long enough to finish only the "Double Eagle," a one-ounce gold piece whose face value was $20. It was first issued in 1907.

On the obverse of the coin is Liberty striding forward. She's a close relative to Sherman's Victory. On the reverse is a soaring eagle (Ill. 80). These coins still come on the market for between $5,000 and $20,000, depending on the condition. (The gold itself is worth about $1,200.)

Roosevelt said of the Double Eagle, "It is simply splendid. I suppose I shall be impeached for it in Congress but I shall regard that as a very cheap payment."

Impeached? For a coin?

Yes: and for something we can't even see. In order to reduce clutter in the design, Saint Gaudens omitted the motto "In God We Trust." During the Civil War, a Pennsylvania minister campaigned to have

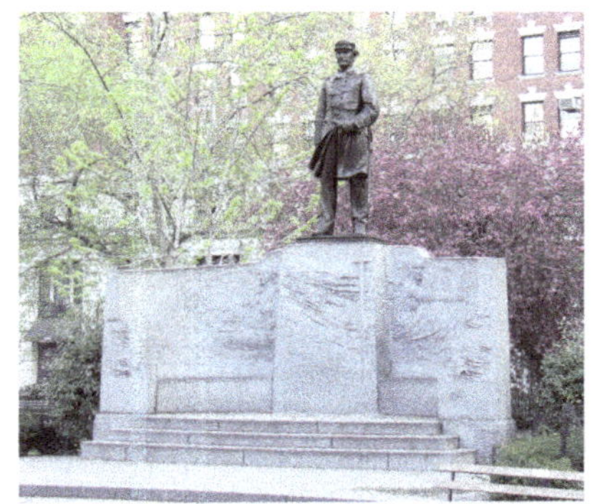

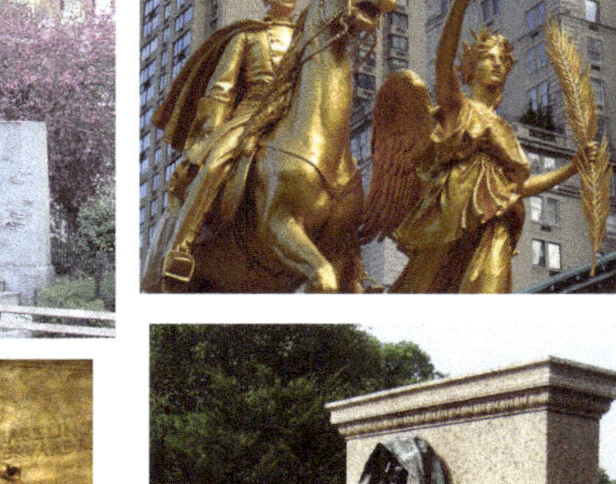

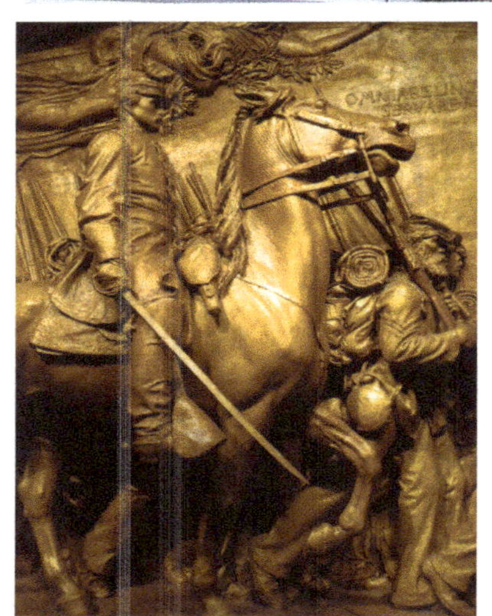

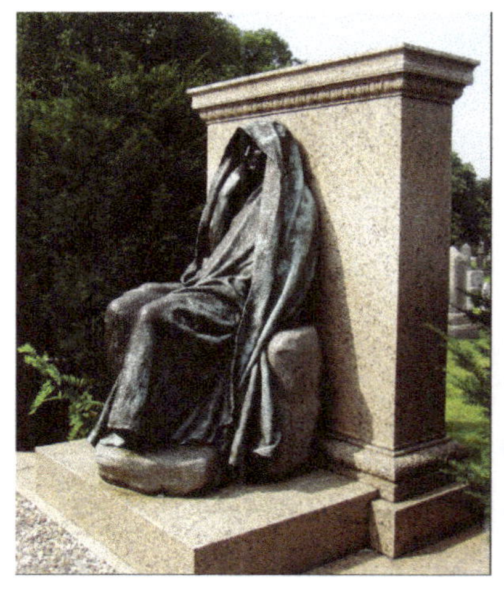

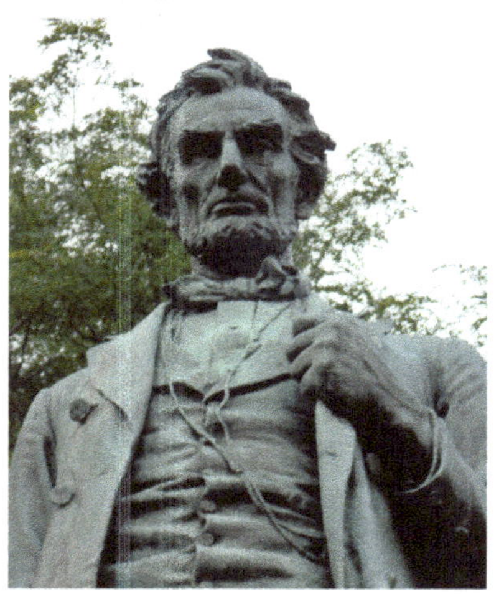

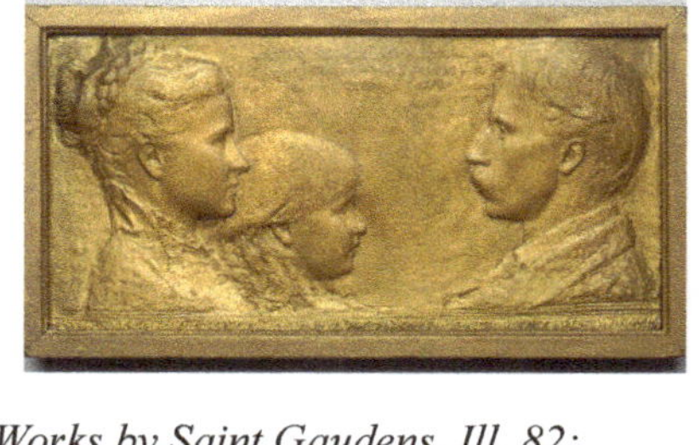

Works by Saint Gaudens. Ill. 82: Farragut, 1880. Ill. 83: Sherman, 1903. Ill. 84: Shaw Memorial, 1897. Ill. 82, 83, 84: photos copyright © 2019 Dianne L. Durante.
Ill. 85: Adams Memorial, 1891; Danevera_1 / Wikipedia. Ill. 86: Lincoln, 1887; Johnym1_2 / Wikipedia. Ill. 87: Gilders family, 1879; MetMuseum.org.

God's name on American coinage, arguing that if the Union ceased to exist, "Antiquaries of succeeding centuries [might] rightly reason ... that we were a heathen nation." In 1864 Congress authorized the use of the motto "In God We Trust" on American coins (Ill. 77-79) ... but as Roosevelt discovered, Congress did not *require* that it be included.

Such was the outcry from clergymen and women's groups about the motto's absence from the new Double Eagle that Roosevelt caved in to pressure. The motto appears on Double Eagles issued after July 1, 1908 (Ill. 81).

SAINT GAUDENS: EVALUATION

Saint Gaudens died of stomach cancer in 1907, at age fifty-nine. He was a wealthy man, and until a month before his death, he was still supervising work at his Cornish studio.

What's unique about Saint Gaudens's works?

All his figures are dignified, thoughtful, unafraid. One would expect that of military heroes, but for Saint Gaudens it's also true of children, women, and men who are ill.

In 1897, at age 49, Saint Gaudens wrote:

> In one of my blue fits the other day ... reasoning about the hopelessness of trying to fathom what it all means, I reached this: we know nothing (of course) but a deep conviction came over me like a flash that at the bottom of it all, whatever it is, the mystery must be beneficent; it doesn't seem ... something malevolent. And the thought was a great comfort." (Wilkinson, *Uncommon Clay*, p. 224)

Saint Gaudens didn't pretend to understand the universe, but he thought it was benevolent. That explains a good deal about the sense of life shown in his sculptures.

I've talked in *Getting More Enjoyment from Art You Love* (available as a Kindle book) about evaluating a specific work of sculpture. It's also possible to evaluate an artist based on his body of work: how original he is with respect to style or subject, and how well he executes his ideas.

As an artist, Saint Gaudens is of very high caliber. He develops new themes and has a distinctive style. As a man, he has an admirable sense of life: he sees the universe as benevolent and man as dignified. For me, that makes all his works worth tracking down. More on how to do that in Chapter 5.

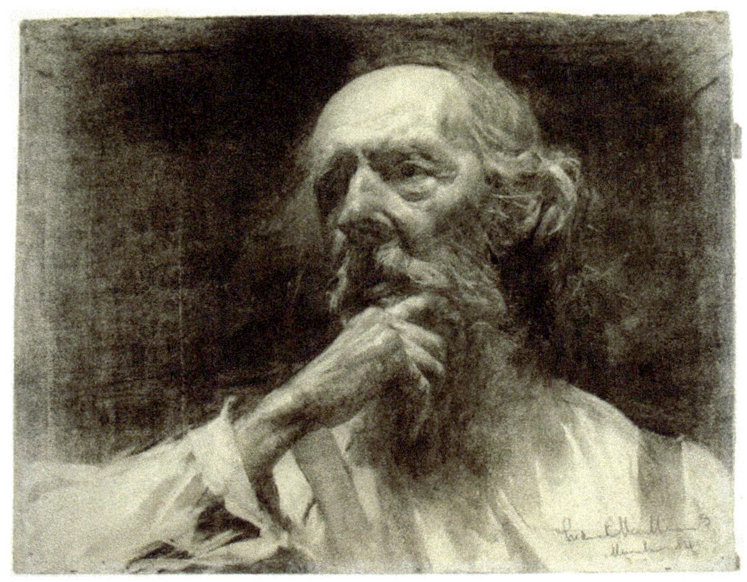

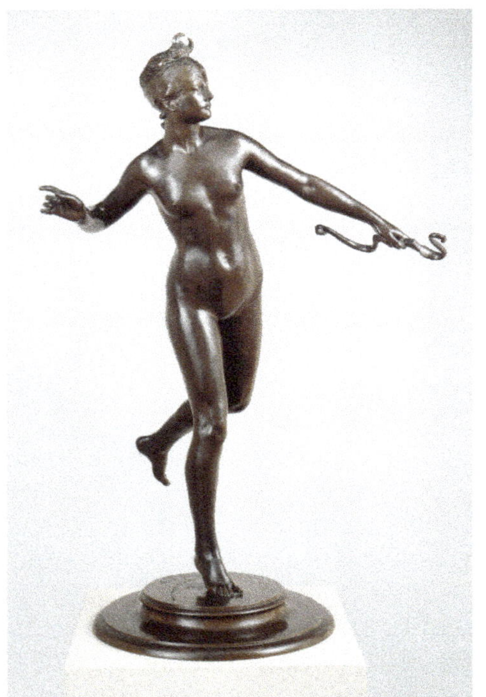

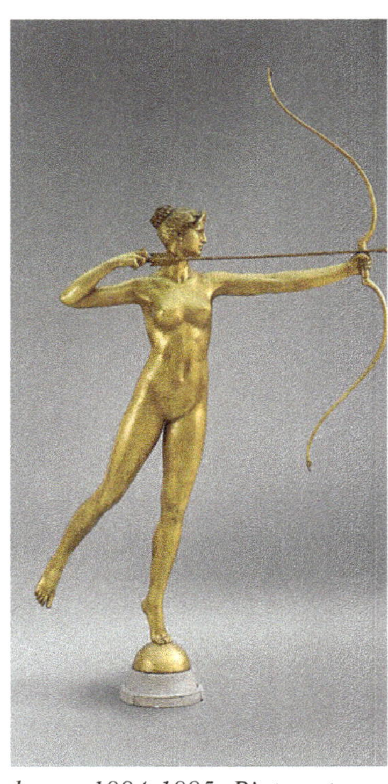

Ill. 89: MacMonnies, Drawing of a bearded man, 1884-1885; Pinterest.
Ill. 90: MacMonnies, Diana, 1888-1889; this cast, 1890; MetMuseum.org.
Ill. 91: Saint Gaudens, Diana, 1891; this reduction, 1894 or later;
MetMuseum.org.

CHAPTER 3
Frederick MacMonnies

Frederick MacMonnies was fifteen years younger than Saint Gaudens. Born in Brooklyn in 1863, he was the son of a wealthy merchant; but his father's business failed, and at age thirteen, MacMonnies left school to earn a living. By age seventeen, he was apprenticed to Saint Gaudens. In Saint Gaudens's studio, MacMonnies modelled forms, enlarged sketches, and worked on lettering for inscriptions. At night, he took drawing classes.

In his early twenties, MacMonnies studied in Paris and Munich. He took more drawing classes and sketched from ancient sculptures (Ill. 89). So like Saint Gaudens, MacMonnies had a thorough knowledge of drawing, sculpting, anatomy, and ancient and modern sculpture.

DIANA, 1890

Sculptures of the goddess Diana by MacMonnies and Saint Gaudens—created a year apart—epitomize the differences between these two artists. MacMonnies's *Diana* was created as a stand-alone piece for exhibition at the Paris Salon (Ill. 90). It's a virtuoso work full of movement and energy, with a complex pose and outline. Saint Gaudens's *Diana,* which was set atop Madison Square Garden a year later, is austere (Ill. 91). It has a simple, easy-to-read outline, suitable for viewing from thirty-two stories below. They're both wonderful works, but they have very different styles and moods.

HALE, 1893

MacMonnies's first widely known work was an image of Nathan Hale for New York's City Hall Park (Ill. 92-95). The commission was awarded to thirty-year-old MacMonnies at the urging of Saint

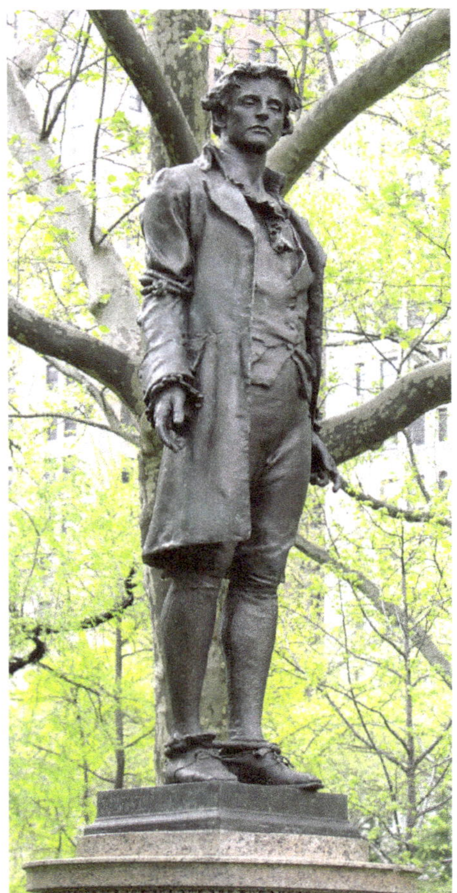

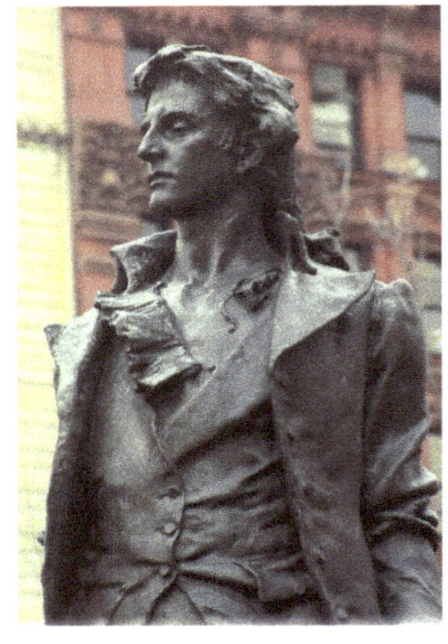

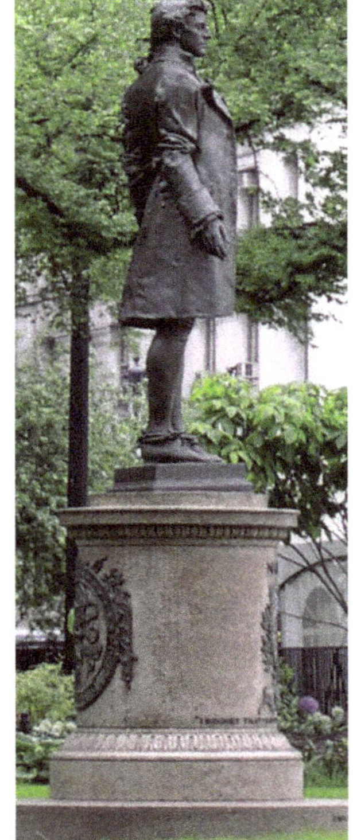

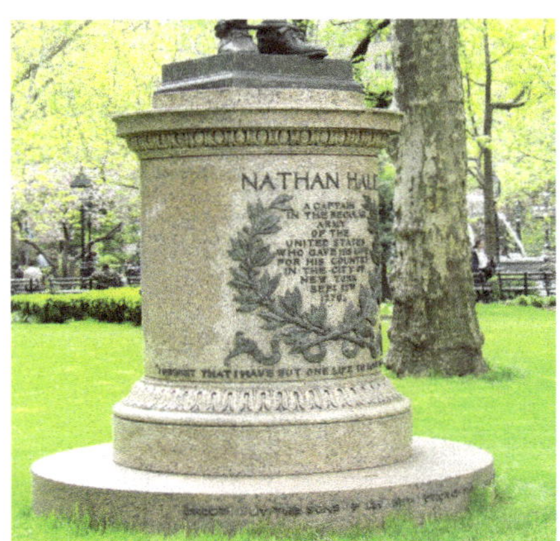

Ill. 92-95: MacMonnies, Nathan Hale, 1893.
Photos copyright © 2019 Dianne L. Durante

Gaudens. Hale, a school-teacher, was twenty-one in 1776, when he was executed as a spy by the British. No portrait of him is known. The committee in charge of the sculpture described what they wanted from MacMonnies:

> a standing fig of a well-built young man of American type, dressed in a simple costume of the end of the last Century ... at the moment immediately preceding his execution by the British, when his well-remembered words, "Would I had more than one life to give for my Country," were uttered. —Quoted in Smart, *A Flight to Fame*, p. 86

MacMonnies created a work far beyond what the committee required—an imaginative, idealized version of Hale. He said:

> I wanted to make something that would set the bootblacks and little clerks around there thinking, something that would make them want to be somebody and find life worth living. —Quoted in Gayle and Cohen, *The Art Commission and the Municipal Art Society Guide to Manhattan's Outdoor Sculpture*, p. 41

How did he do that? By a combination of posture, expression, and costume. *Hale* stands tall, shoulders back, tense. The long verticals of his coat and the snug vest and pants emphasize his slender body. His chin is lifted and his hands gesture. But he's frowning slightly, head turned aside, eyelids lowered. He looks disdainful. Why?

When we look more carefully, we see that ropes bind his elbows and ankles. The neck of his shirt has been torn open so the executioner can put a noose around it. *Hale* is a captive about to be hanged. Yet he disdains his captors and his fate.

How does one achieve such defiance—such disdain for imminent death? By the certainty that one is fighting for the right, even if one is not winning. It's defiance that made Nathan Hale famous, not the mere fact of his death; and defiance is what's shown here.

MacMonnies's *Hale* is an inspiration to the bootblacks, the clerks, and the rest of us not because MacMonnies showed life, liberty, and the pursuit of happiness—the specific values that Hale fought for. It's an inspiration because MacMonnies showed the *way* in which Hale fought for those values: steadfastly, courageously, defiantly. That makes *Hale* a model not only for those who shared his values, but for all those who aspire to difficult goals.

MacMonnies was working in France in 1893, when *Hale* was dedicated. Saint Gaudens supervised the placement of the sculpture in

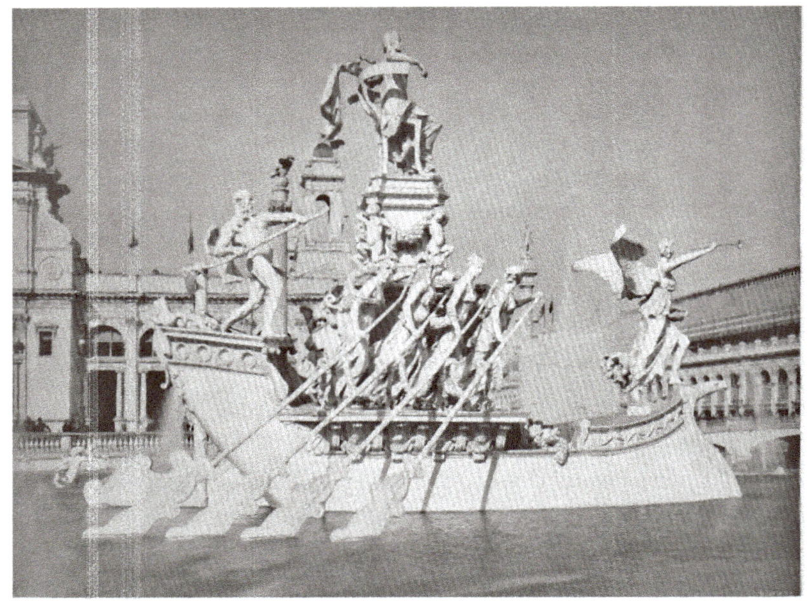

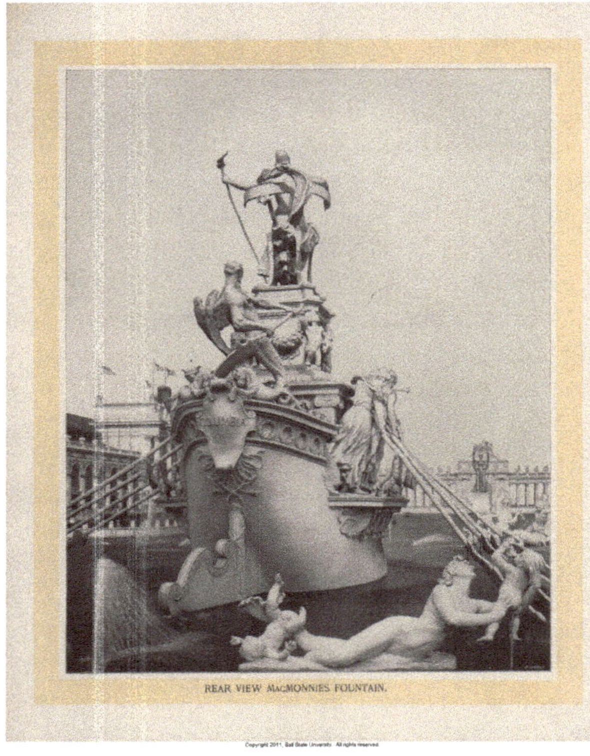

Ill. 96-97: MacMonnies, Ship of State, 1893. Wikipedia.

City Hall Park. Once the sculpture was on its pedestal, Saint Gaudens decided he didn't like the angle of the figure, and inserted a one-and-a-half-inch wedge under *Hale's* toes, to tilt him back. The slant of the pedestal is visible in Ill. 95.

A mere ten years earlier, MacMonnies had been Saint Gaudens's studio assistant, and they had a difficult time reaching an equal relationship. In this case, Saint Gaudens wrote to MacMonnies explaining that he'd added the wedge to *Hale*, and said if MacMonnies didn't like it, he'd have a derrick come and lift the sculpture so the wedge could be pulled out. MacMonnies chose not to insist.

Nathan Hale is one of my favorite sculptures in New York City. In my opinion, if an artist does even one piece of sculpture of this quality, he deserves thanks and fame throughout the ages.

SHIP OF STATE, 1893

MacMonnies's *Ship of State* was one of the centerpieces of the Columbian Exposition in 1893-1894 (Ill. 96-97). The huge ship, fifty feet long, bore eight rowers and three passengers. Father Time, steering at the back, was eighteen feet high. In front of the barge were eight seahorses; behind was a semi-circle of dolphins. The circular base was one hundred fifty feet in diameter—half the size of a football field. It was the largest fountain in the world.

The *Ship of State* captured the American spirit of pride and celebration. Photos of it appeared in newspapers and magazines across the country. Like all the outdoor sculpture and buildings at the Exposition, it was made of perishable materials, and is long gone … but twenty million people saw it. It made MacMonnies famous nationwide.

BACCHANTE AND INFANT FAUN, 1894

MacMonnies became famous with the *Ship of State*—and notorious with *Bacchante and Infant Faun,* completed the year the Exposition closed (Ill. 98-100). The sculpture shows a woman balanced on one foot. There's a joyful, spiraling line upward to the baby on her arm and the bunch of grapes in her other hand. According to MacMonnies's title, she's a Bacchante—a follower of Bacchus or Dionysus, god of wine. The baby is a faun, another follower of Dionysus. His fascinated gaze shows his early love of grapes.

I love this sculpture for a feature that's very difficult to capture in a photograph: the look on the baby's face. His eyes are wide, and his mouth is just beginning to turn up into a smile (Ill. 100). He looks like

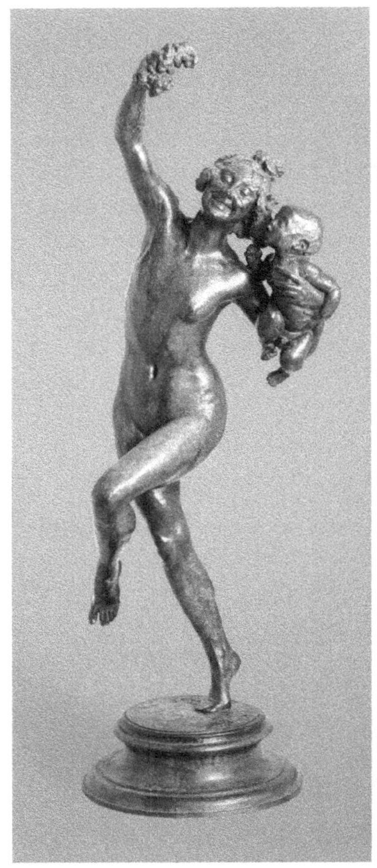

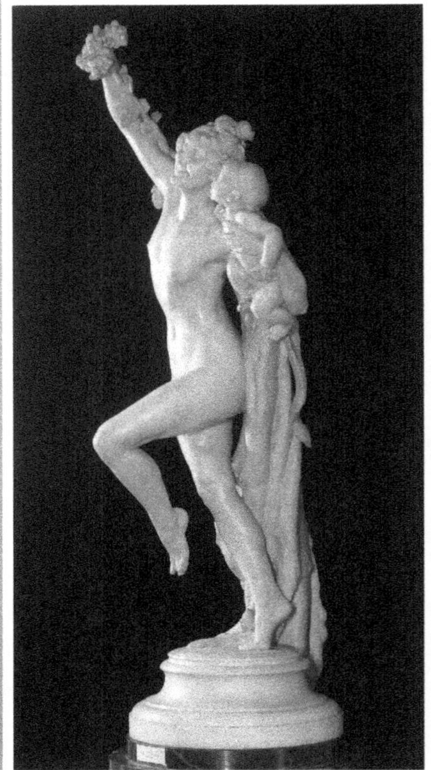

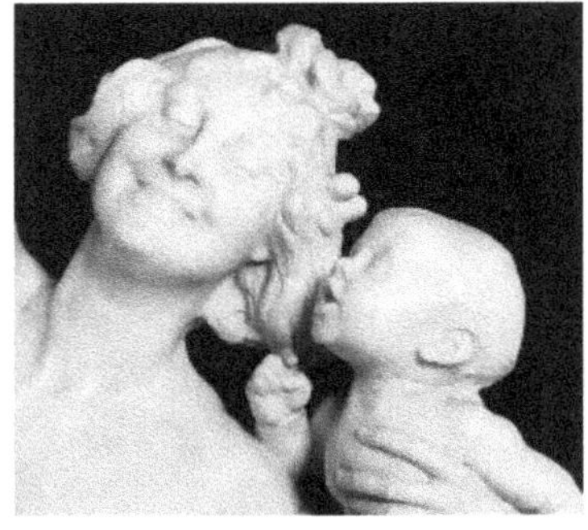

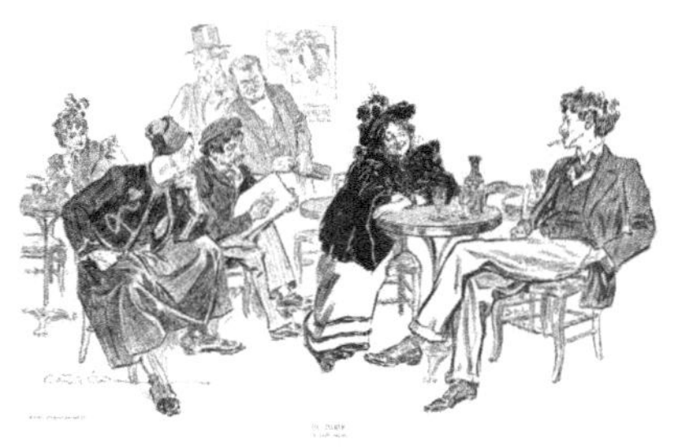

MacMonnies, Bacchante with Infant Faun, 1894.
Ill. 98: Bronze; photo MetMuseum.org. Ill. 99-100: Marble; photos
Brooklyn Museum. Ill. 101: Gibson, Cafe Artists, 1894. MacMonnies is at
the far right; his model faces him across the table.

he's thinking: "I want those! I can *get* those!" It's the closest I've ever seen to "radiant greed" in a sculpture.

MacMonnies gave the *Bacchante* to Charles McKim, a noted architect who had hired MacMonnies early in his career. McKim donated the sculpture to Boston Public Library, which he had designed. This was two years after Saint Gaudens's *Diana* was raised atop Madison Square Garden in New York City and was well liked (Ill. 56-60).

But in Boston, a group of residents were scandalized by the *Bacchante*. She was naked, they said. She was drunk: the title said so. Even worse: she was not an austere, idealized figure like Saint Gaudens's *Diana*. She was a recognizable portrait of one of MacMonnies's French models (Ill. 101).

The *Bacchante* was installed at Boston Public Library, but protests continued. McKim finally withdrew his gift and presented it to the Metropolitan Museum of Art in New York, which is why it's in the American Wing there.

MACMONNIES AS ENTREPRENEUR

Following in Saint Gaudens's footsteps, MacMonnies sold reductions (reduced-size copies) of his works. In the 1890s, Tiffany's offered the *Bacchante* in 34-inch, 24-inch, and 18-inch sizes.

From commissions and the sale of reductions, MacMonnies had an annual estimated income during the 1890s of around $300,000. In 2019 dollars, that would be about more than $7.5 million. As his biographer notes, it was "a great deal of money, joyfully spent" (Smart, *Flight to Fame*, p. ix).

PARIS INTERNATIONAL EXPOSITION OF 1900

The high point of MacMonnies's career came in 1900, when the International Exposition in Paris had on display several of his major works: the *Bacchante,* the pair of *Horse Tamers* for Prospect Park, Brooklyn (1898; Ill. 102), and the groups representing the Army and the Navy for the arch at Grand Army Plaza in Brooklyn (1901; Ill. 103-105).

Also on display at the International Exposition in 1900 was Saint Gaudens's plaster model for *Sherman*. And just outside the fairgrounds was a pavilion dedicated to the works of Auguste Rodin. Rodin's works were acclaimed by the critics, and his pavilion was subsidized by the

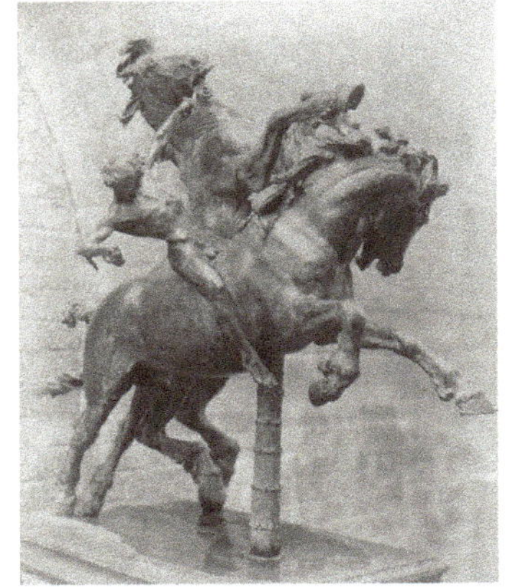

Ill. 102: MacMonnies, Horse Tamers, 1898. Prospect Park, Brooklyn. Image: Smithsonian Institution Research Information System (SIRIS).

Ill. 103-105: Soldiers' and Sailors' Arch, 1901. Grand Army Plaza, Brooklyn. Photos copyright © 2019 Dianne L. Durante

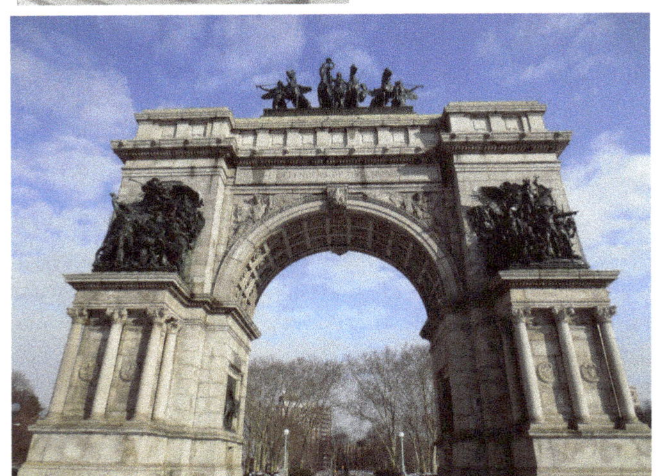

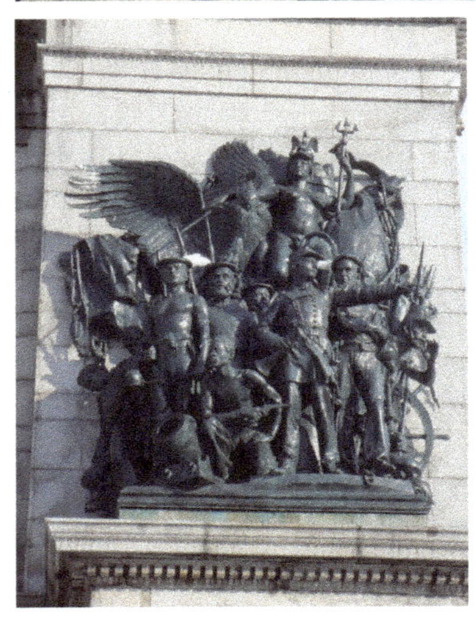

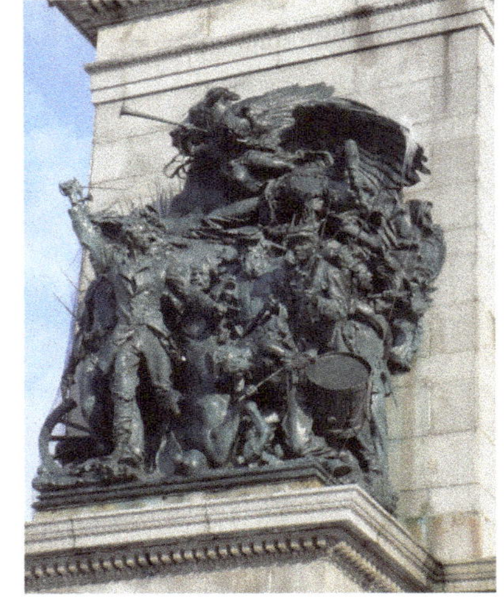

city of Paris. This did not bode well for the future of representational sculpture, but it wasn't immediately relevant to MacMonnies. For more on Rodin's career and his influence, see *Innovators in Sculpture.*

MACMONNIES AS PAINTER

Creating large-scale bronzes required major funding and usually working with committees. Over the years MacMonnies had had many problems with such committees. On the other hand, he had painted in oils for more than a decade, and he liked using color. In the same year as the International Exposition, MacMonnies announced that he was temporarily giving up sculpture for painting.

MacMonnies painted competent portraits in a style influenced by the Impressionists. (Ill. 106-108; that's his second wife in Ill. 108.) But he never made as much money painting as he had sculpting. By 1904, he had returned to sculpting.

BEAUTY AND TRUTH, 1920

For the magnificent Fifth Avenue façade of New York Public Library, MacMonnies created two fountain sculptures, begun in 1914 and placed in 1920. Most people who've seen the façade don't even remember that they flank the stairs to the main entrance (Ill. 109-111).

One is a simpering female, the other a tired old man. At first MacMonnies called them "Philosophy" and "Thought"; later he renamed them "Beauty" and "Truth". Without the inscriptions, they'd

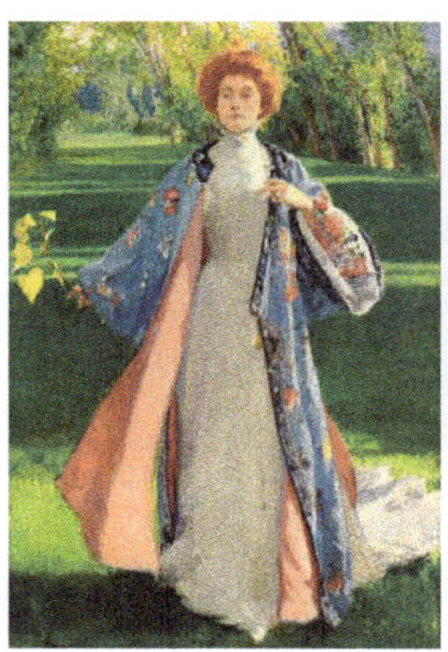
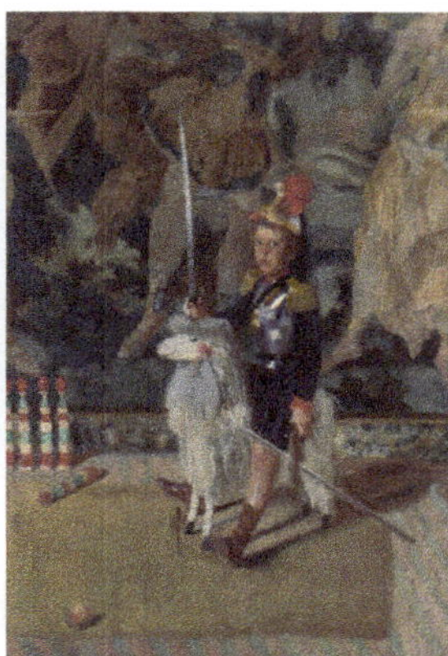
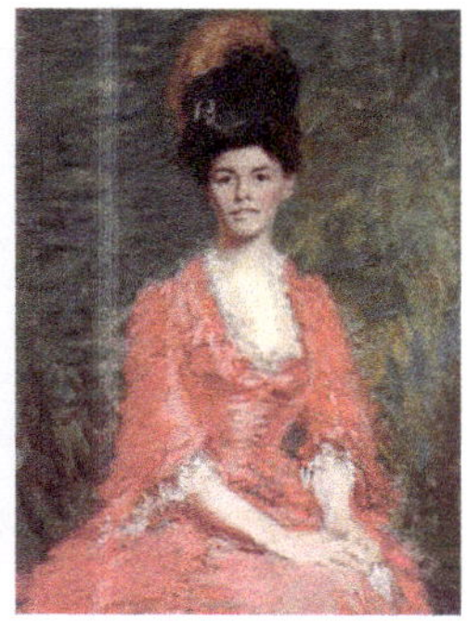

MacMonnies portraits. Ill. 106: May Suydam Palmer, 1901. Pinterest.
Ill. 107: Young Chevalier, 1898. Pinterest.
Ill. 108: Alice MacMonnies, ca. 1910. Ex-Terra Museum.

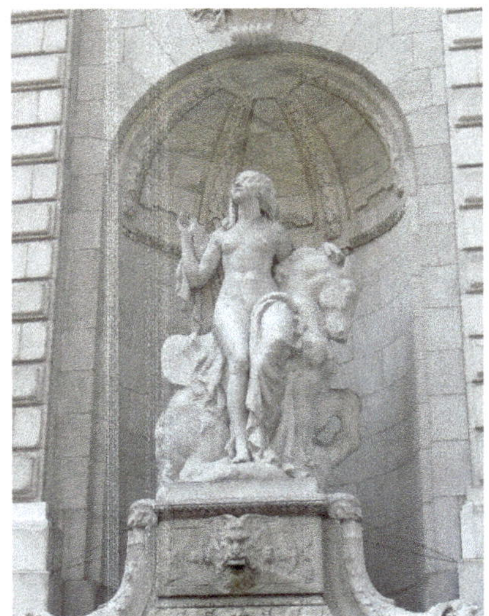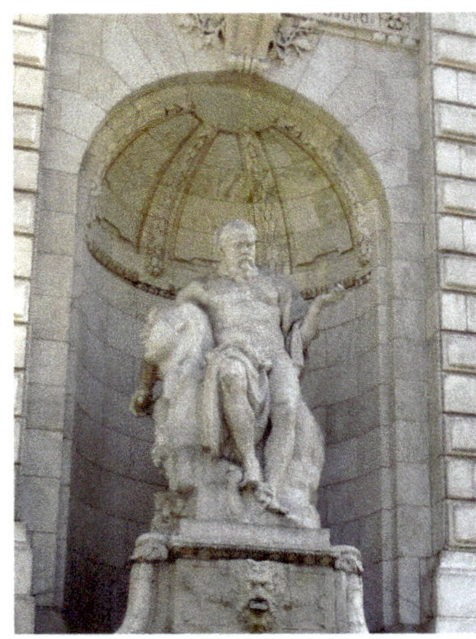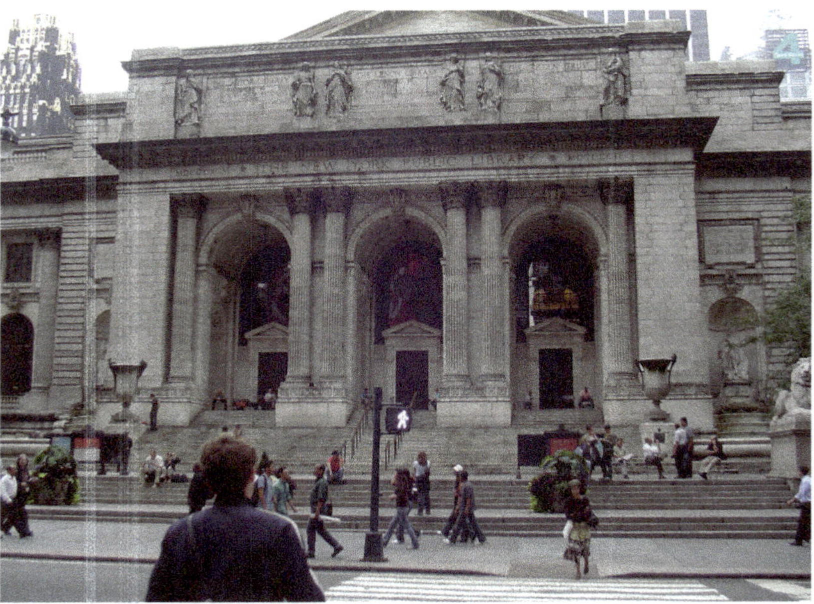

Ill. 109-111: MacMonnies, Beauty and Truth, 1920. New York Public Library, Fifth Avenue at 42nd St. Ill. 109-110: Photos copyright © 2019 Dianne L. Durante. Ill. 111: Gustavo Morales Diaz / Wikipedia

be unidentifiable. As works of art, that makes them weak. It's difficult to believe they're the work of the same man who created *Nathan Hale* twenty years earlier.

CIVIC VIRTUE, 1922

The next work is a good illustration of the importance of a sculpture's setting—and the limits of what setting can do. Based on the details, let's see if we can figure out what the work in Ill. 112-117 represents.

The man is fifteen feet tall. He's young, strong, and confident, but rather heavy. He doesn't look as if he's in motion or even energetic. His face is serious or expressionless. A sword is balanced on his shoulder. Behind his back (Ill. 115) he holds something twisty: a rope? a plant? Even in person, that's not clear.

At his feet are two figures with women's torsos. Instead of legs, they have scaly tails that twine around the man's legs without actually touching him. One has an octopus for hair. The other holds a skull with a finger through one eye (Ill. 114). Near them, at the man's feet, is a shipwreck. These figures clearly represent something evil, something dangerous to humans …but it's not clear what.

All we can figure out from observing the sculpture is that this is a strong man triumphing over something evil.

According to MacMonnies, this sculpture represents the "Triumph of Civic Virtue": good politics (the strong young man) triumphing over graft and corruption (the evil mermaids). In the man's hand is the

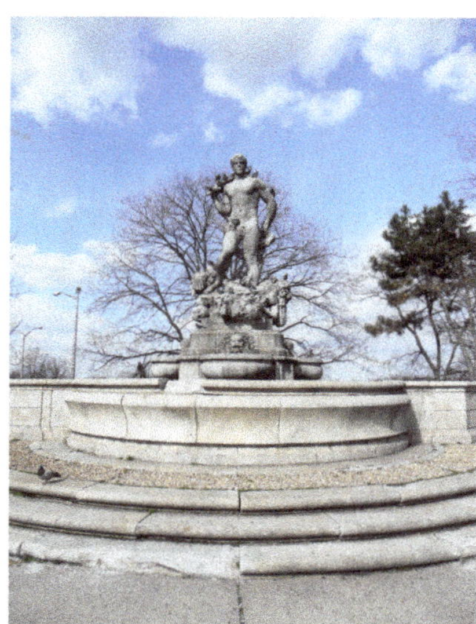

Ill. 112: MacMonnies, Civic Virtue, 1922, in its former location near Queens County Courthouse. Photo copyright © 2019 Dianne L. Durante

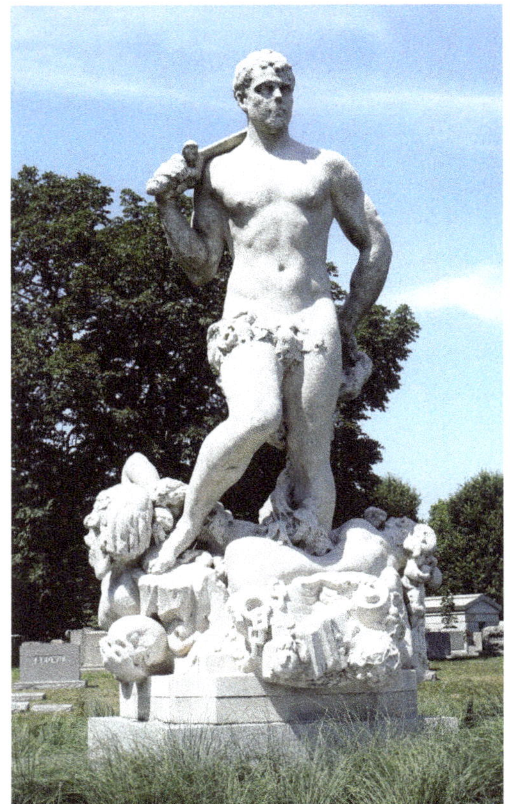

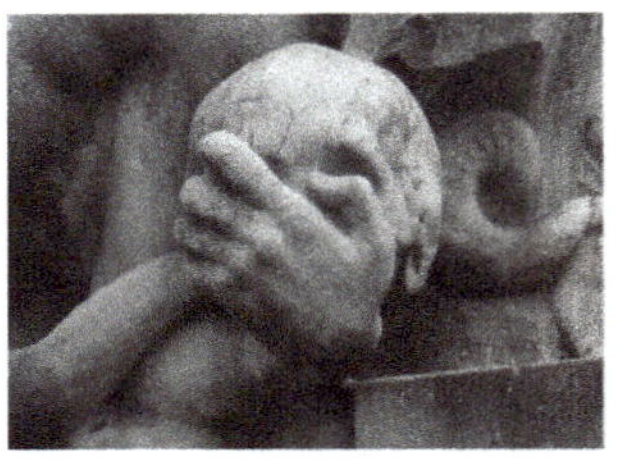

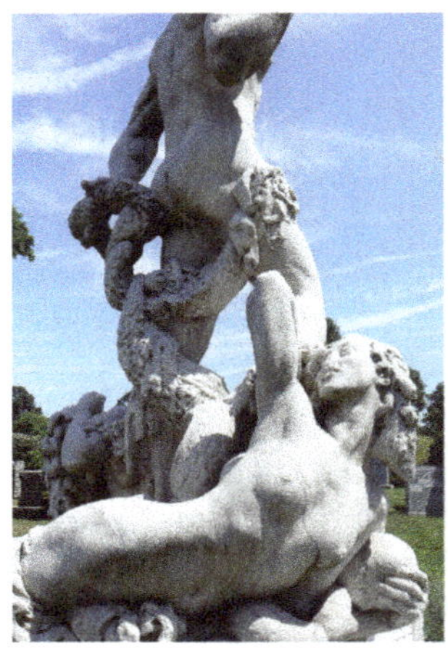

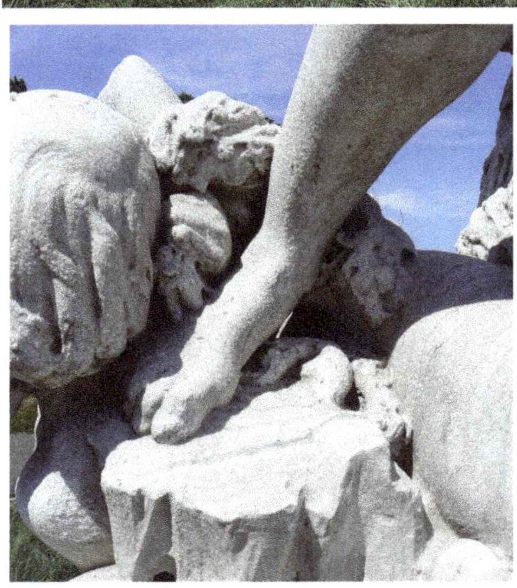

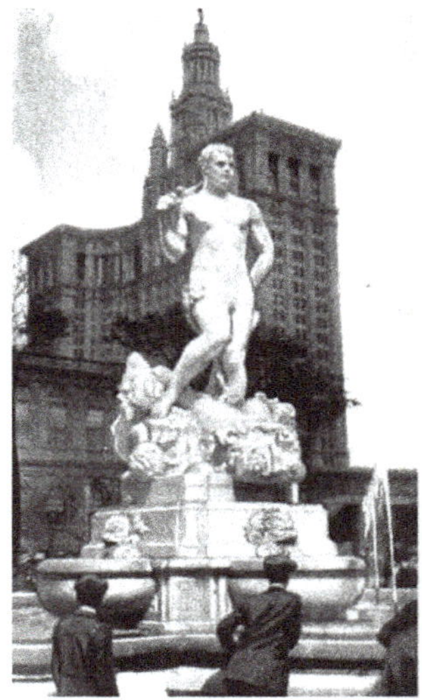

Ill. 113-117: MacMonnies,
Civic Virtue, 1922.
Ill. 116 Wikipedia.
Other photos copyright ©
2019 Dianne L. Durante

net with which the mermaids hoped to ensnare him. He's stepping up and away from them—they don't touch him.

New York City politics in the late nineteenth century was notoriously corrupt: it was the era of Tammany Hall and Boss Tweed. (See Chapter 8 in *Central Park: The Early Years.*) By the early twentieth century, such politicians had much less influence. *Civic Virtue* was designed to stand in front of City Hall, to congratulate politicians and to remind them to stay on the virtuous path.

MacMonnies was capable of excellent work, but *Civic Virtue* is not one of his best. It doesn't convey its message clearly and unequivocally, even in its original setting. And it's no longer in its original setting, because this sculpture became highly controversial.

MacMonnies began *Civic Virtue* in 1909, before World War I. He finished it in 1922. Meanwhile, in 1920, the Nineteenth Amendment was passed, granting women the right to vote. John Hylan, mayor of New York—thinking of all those new votes—showed a photo of *Civic Virtue* to a number of women before the sculpture was set in place. They were outraged. How sexist! A man trampling women!

Of course, they're not women and the man is not trampling them. But why let truth get in the way of a political rant?

Despite the controversy, *Civic Virtue* was set up in 1922 in a large fountain in front of City Hall (Ill. 116). But in 1941, Mayor Fiorello La Guardia and Parks Commissioner Robert Moses banished *Civic Virtue* to the outer boroughs. For several decades it stood on the same block as the Queens County Courthouse, although it was too far away for the connection with government to be obvious. The sculpture was still often condemned as sexist, and the politically correct politicians of Queens refused to allocate money for maintenance. By the time the twenty-first century rolled in, the sculpture was vandalized and disintegrating, covered with pigeons and pigeon droppings.

In 2012 *Civic Virtue* was suddenly and without fanfare moved to the Green-Wood Cemetery in Brooklyn. The basin was left in Queens, so the figure looks bereft, if one knows the original setting. But at least it's been cleaned and repaired (Ill. 113).

In my opinion, it's not the government's proper business to commission or own sculptures. (See my essay "Portraits and Public Sculptures" at https://diannedurantewriter.com/archives/4121). If the government owns sculptures and is unwilling to maintain them, it should sell them rather than letting them crumble to dust. I don't like *Civic Virtue,* but I'm glad it's found a home at Green-Wood.

MACMONNIES'S LATER CAREER

Partly due to the uproar over *Civic Virtue,* MacMonnies refused to take on any new public commissions in the 1920s. He did finish two major works, the *Princeton Battle Monument* in Princeton, New Jersey, dedicated 1922 (Ill. 118), and the *Marne Battle Monument,* dedicated in 1932 in Meaux, France.

Looking at these, the groups and the Soldiers' and Sailors' Arch (Ill. 103-105), *Truth* and *Beauty* at New York Public Library (Ill. 109-110), and *Civic Virtue* (Ill. 112-117), as compared to *Nathan Hale* and the *Bacchante* (Ill. 92-95, 98-100), it's clear that MacMonnies was much better at single figures than grand allegorical compositions.

But aside from MacMonnies's dislike for working with committees, there was another reason that MacMonnies's production of sculpture tapered off. The City Beautiful movement with its classical

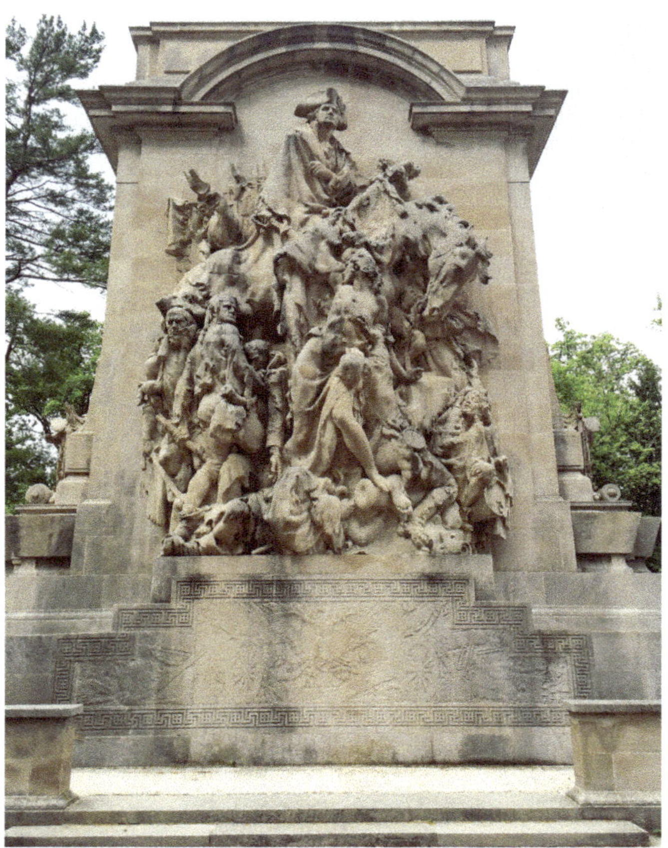

Ill. 118: MacMonnies, Princeton Battle Monument, 1922.
Djkeddie_2 / Wikipedia

architecture reigned supreme for the thirty years following the Columbian Exposition of 1893-1894. (See p. 13.) After that, Art Deco architecture began coming into fashion. Art Deco buildings had far less sculptural decoration than buildings in the classical style. *Civic Virtue,* dedicated in 1922, was one of the last large allegorical sculptures erected in New York City.

In the 1890s and early 1900s, MacMonnies lived lavishly in France. Later he lived lavishly in New York City, until the stock market crash in 1929. During his years in New York he produced some small works, such as a bust of the painter James Abbott McNeill Whistler (Ill. 119).

When MacMonnies died in 1937 of pneumonia, he had produced no major works for a decade or so. The newspapers wrote of him in glowing terms after his death.

MACMONNIES: EVALUATION

What's the distinguishing characteristic of MacMonnies's works? That changes over the course of his career. In the 1890s, his works are full of energy (graceful, tense, or violent), and show innovation and remarkable technical skill. In the early twentieth century, his work trailed off into rather boring, uninspired pieces.

Given the quality of MacMonnies's later work, I can't rank him as an artist as high as I do Saint Gaudens. But his *Nathan Hale* and *Bacchante* are two of my favorite sculptures of all time.

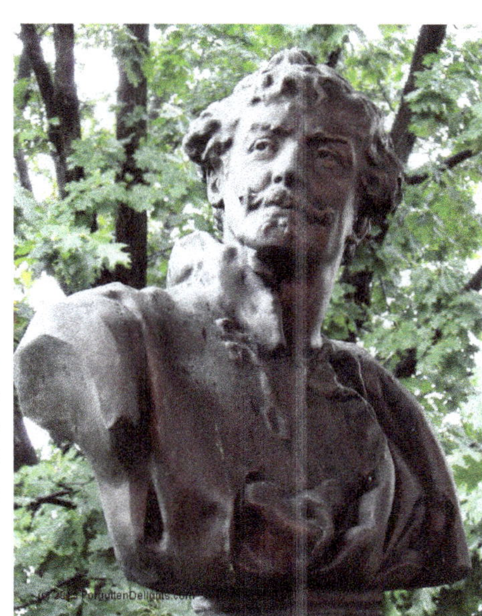

Ill. 119: MacMonnies, Whistler, 1930. Hall of Fame of Great Americans, Bronx. Photo copyright © 2019 Dianne L. Durante

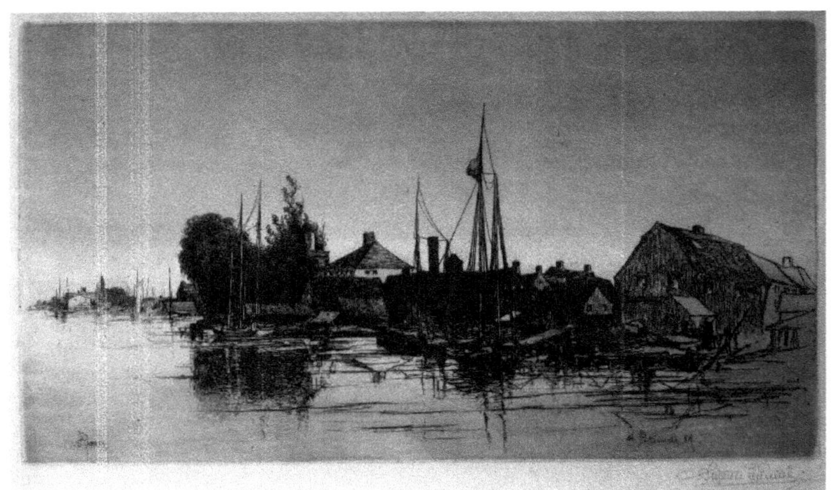

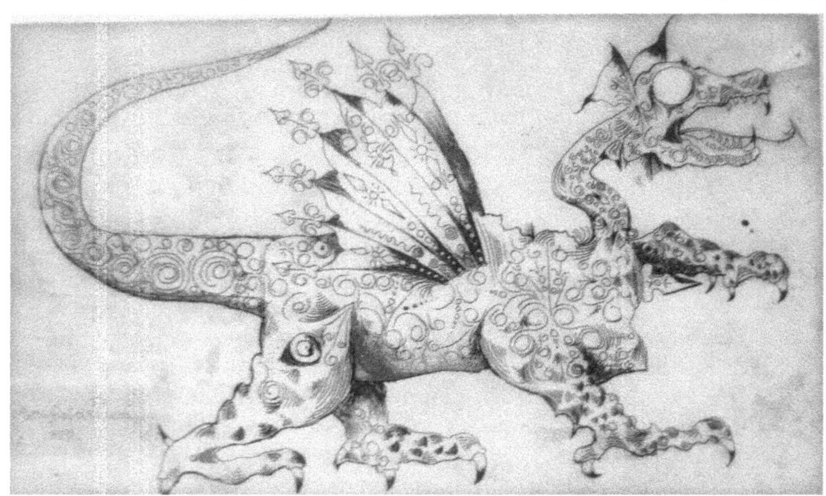

Ill. 120: Etching by Stephen Parrish, 1884. Brooklyn Museum.
Ill. 121: Maxfield Parrish, Sketch of a dragon, 1877.

CHAPTER 4
Maxfield Parrish

Parrish was twenty-two years younger than Saint Gaudens and was only thirty-seven when Saint Gaudens died. But he was a neighbor and friend of Saint Gaudens's in Cornish, New Hampshire, and the two shared a similar sense of life. Like Saint Gaudens and MacMonnies, Parrish worked hard to learn his craft, developed a distinctive style, and made tons of money.

TRAINING AND CONTEXT

Frederick Maxfield Parrish was born in 1870 in Philadelphia. His parents were Quakers, wealthy and of good social standing. Father Stephen was a landscape painter and one of the best etchers in the United States (Ill. 120).

When Frederick was seven, his parents took their only child to Europe. There he saw many things that didn't look at all like Philadelphia: castles, gargoyles, snow-capped mountain peaks. One of Frederick's earliest drawings, a fanciful dragon, was sketched when he was seven years old (Ill. 121).

There's a chicken-and-egg question here. Did seeing castles, gargoyles, and snowy mountains make a lasting impression on young Frederick? Or did he pay attention to such things because they already interested him? After all, he could have focused instead on street scenes, peasant life, or women in high-fashion clothes. Whatever the answers—I don't have them—fantasy and olden-time themes are prominent in Parrish's work for decades.

At age fourteen, in 1884, Frederick went back to Europe with his parents for two years. At the end of that trip, he caught typhoid. Typhoid was life-threatening: in the 1880s in New York City alone, it killed hundreds of people every year. While Frederick was recovering, his father taught him drawing and etching. There's a pattern here.

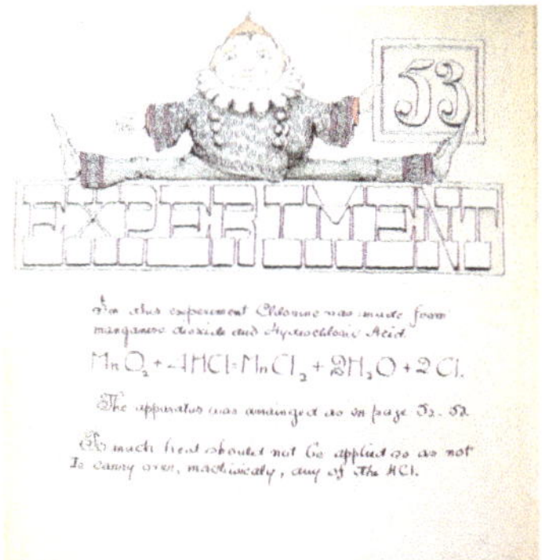

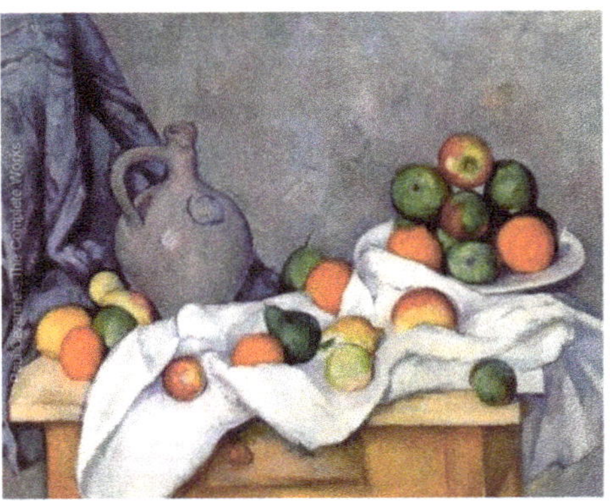

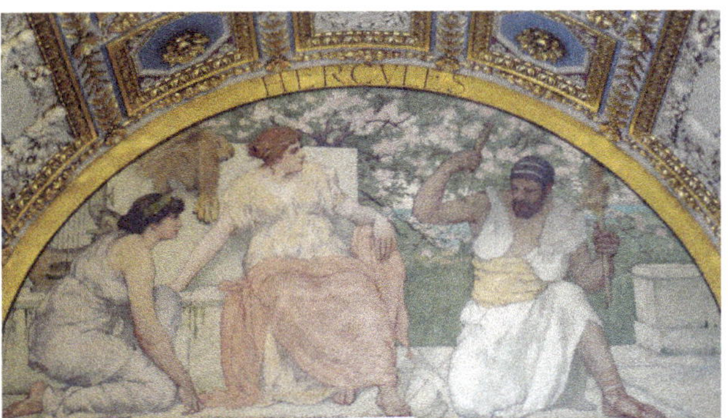

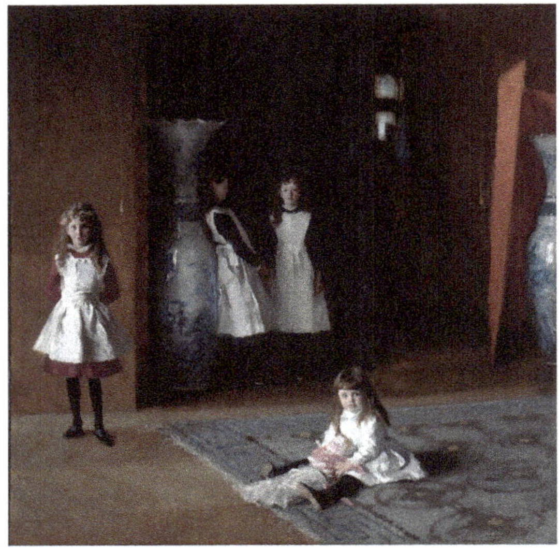

Ill. 122: Parrish, page from chemistry notebook, 1889. Ill. 123: Cezanne, Drapery, Pitcher and Fruit Bowl, 1893-1894. Wikipedia. Ill. 124: William McEwen, Hercules, 1896; Library of Congress. Ill. 125: John Singer Sargent, Daughters of Edward Darley Boit, 1882; Wikipedia.

Parrish didn't have an easy life, but he always made something of the rough spots.

In 1888, soon after his recovery from typhoid, Parrish started attending college to study architecture. The pages of his chemistry notebook suggest that he wasn't into the hard sciences (Ill. 122). Architecture was a false start. In 1892, when he was twenty-two, Parrish enrolled in the best art school in the United States: the Academy of Fine Arts in Philadelphia.

We've already seen what was happening in architecture and sculpture in the 1890s, when Parrish went to school (pp. 11-13). But what about painting?

In the 1890s in Europe, critics were praising Rodin, Monet, Cezanne, and other avant-garde artists (Ill. 123), but that wasn't the public taste in America. When used as architectural decoration, paintings usually showed mythological or allegorical figures in classical drapery, to go with classical architecture (Ill. 124). Painted portraits, usually made as stand-alone works for America's rising middle and upper classes, had realistic, modern costumes and settings (Ill. 125).

But painters had another way to make money besides frescoes, murals, or canvases. In America, the middle class was growing and gaining more leisure. Before the invention of radio and television, the printed word was one of the prime means of entertainment. The 1890s saw the publication of *The Importance of Being Earnest* (Oscar Wilde), *The Turn of the Screw* (Henry James), *The Jungle Book* (Rudyard Kipling), and *Dracula* (Bram Stoker), along with many others.

Also very popular were magazines. During the nineteenth century, the quality of color printing steadily improved. Illustrations sold magazines (Ill. 126-128), so illustrators were celebrities. The period is known as the "Golden Age of Illustration."

Famous illustrators of the 1890s include Howard Pyle, Charles Dana Gibson, and Frederic Remington (Ill.129, 130, 131). Also enormously popular were Edwin Austin Abbey, Jessie Wilcox Smith, and one of my favorites, N.C. Wyeth (Ill. 132, 133, 134). These were the best-known illustrators in the 1890s, when Parrish went to school and began his career. We'll see in a moment that in subject and style, Parrish's work is very different from those of his older contemporaries.

That's the context for 1892, when Parrish enrolled in the Academy of Fine Arts in Philadelphia. He stayed there two and a half years. Among other things, he learned to use costumed models and to use photography for studies. He learned the principles of scientific color

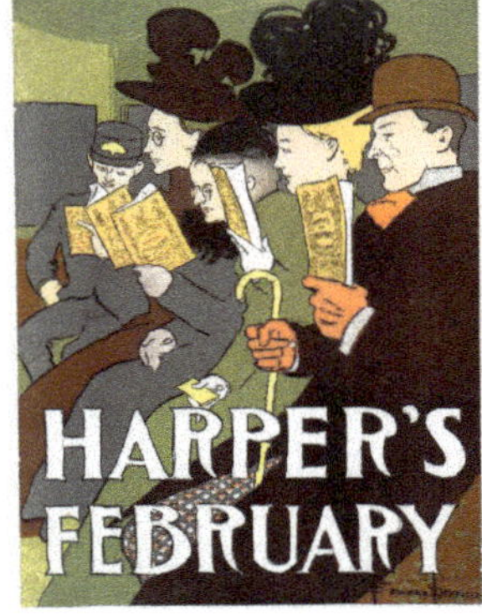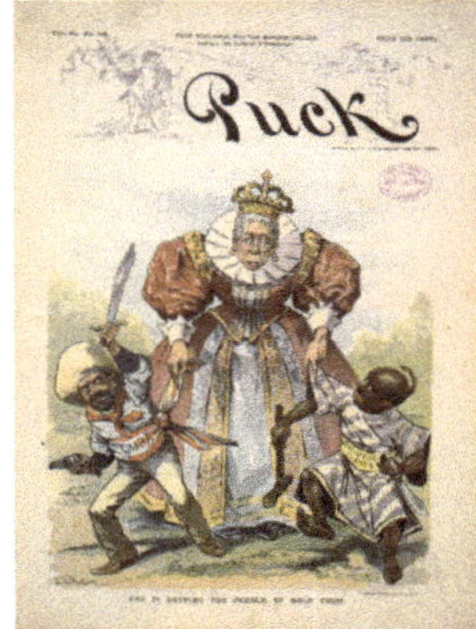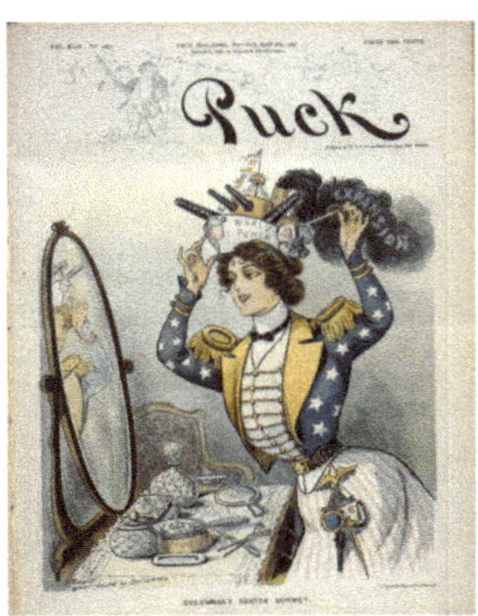

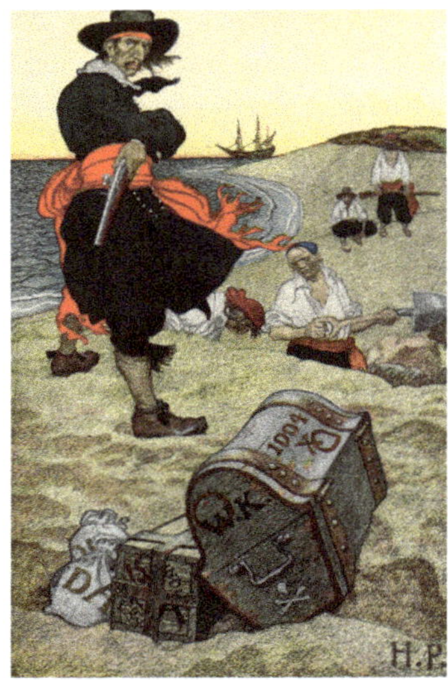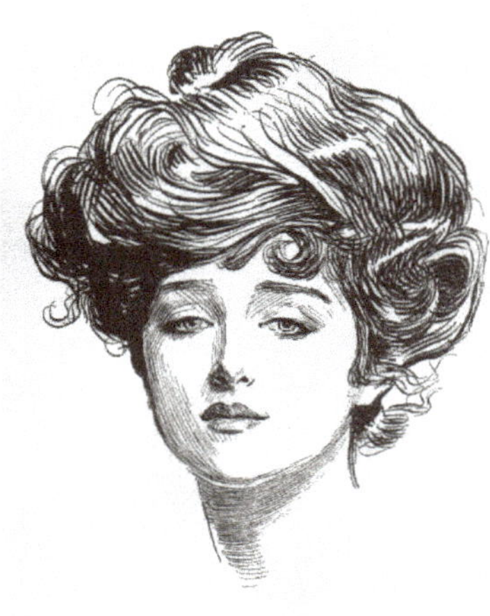

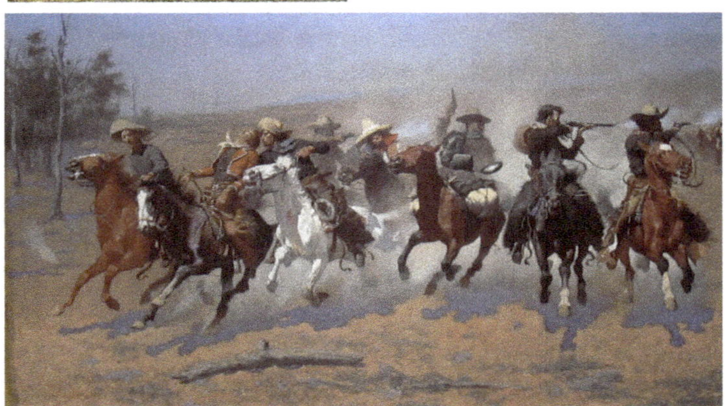

Ill. 126, 127, 128: Magazines of 1895, 1896, 1901.
Ill. 129: Howard Pyle, illustration for The Book of Pirates, 1911; Wikipedia.
Ill. 130: Charles Dana Gibson, a Gibson Girl, ca. 1891; Wikipedia.
Ill. 131: Frederic Remington, A Dash for the Timber, 1889; Wikipedia.

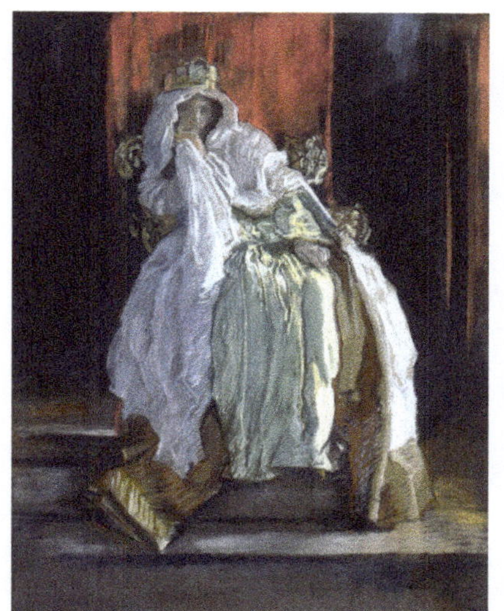

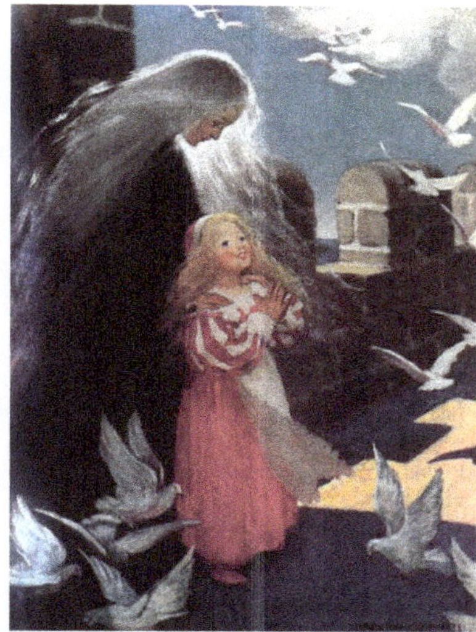

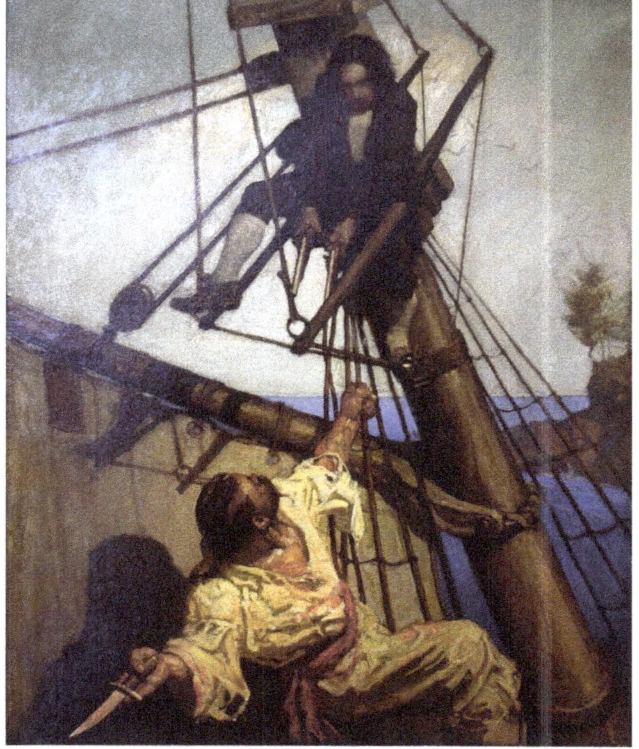

Ill. 132: Edwin Austin Abbey, The Queen in Hamlet, ca. 1897; Wikipedia.
Ill. 133: Jessie Wilcox Smith, illustration for The Princess and
the Goblin, 1920; Wikipedia.
Ill. 134: N.C. Wyeth, illustration for Treasure Island, 1911; Wikipedia.

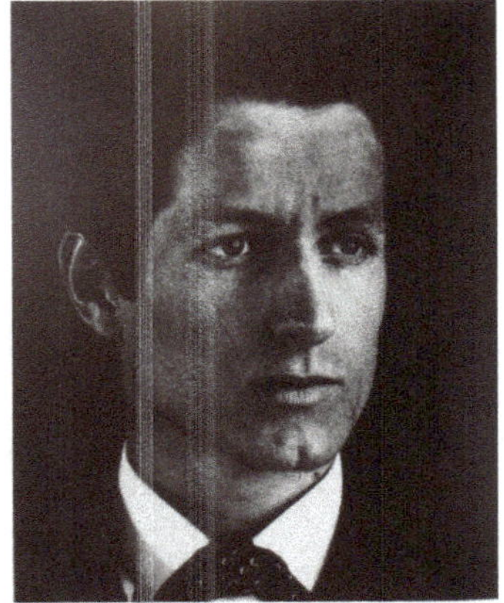

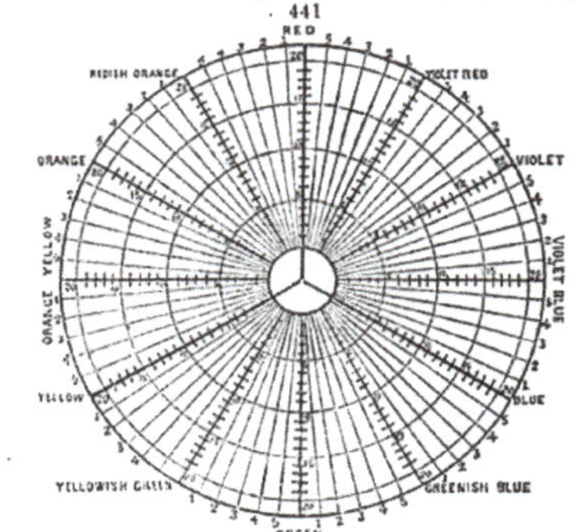

800. Chevreul's classification of colors, and chromatic diagram.—The chromatic diagram, of Chevreul, fig. 441, greatly

facilitates the study of complementary colors, and the modifications produced by their mutual proximity.

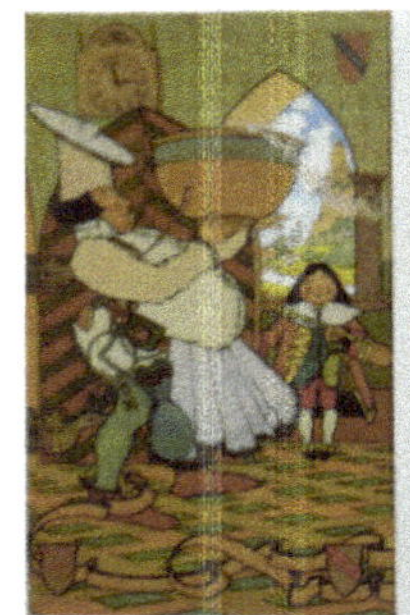

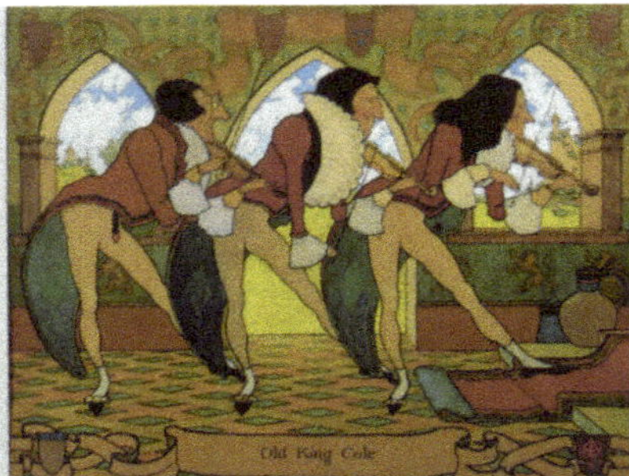

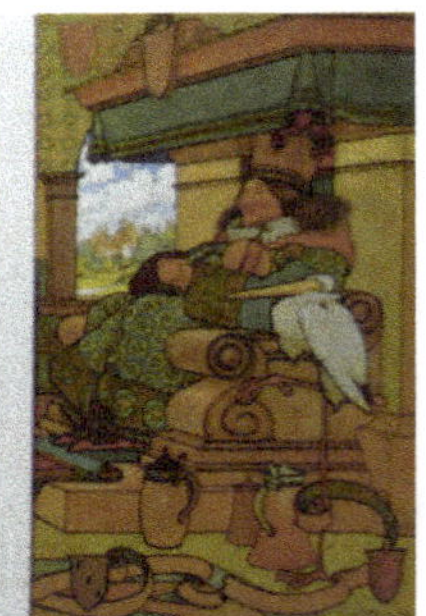

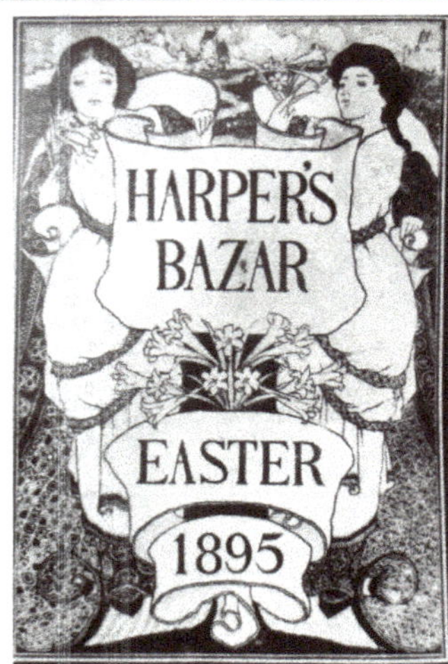

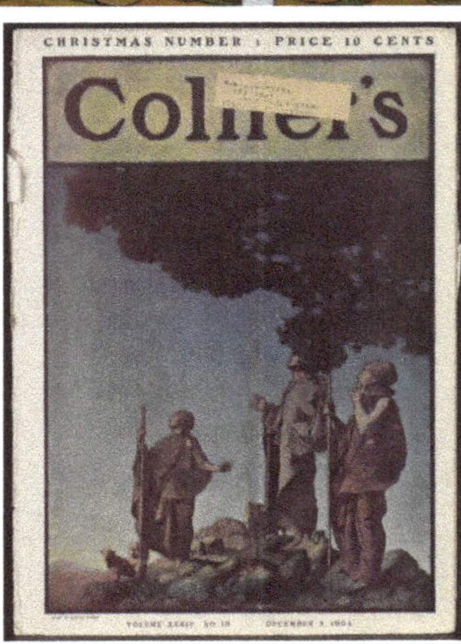

Ill. 135: Parrish in 1896; Wikipedia.
Ill. 136: Color theory wheel from Chevreuil, 1855; Wikipedia.
Ill. 137: Parrish, Old King Cole, 1894; Wikipedia.
Ill. 138: Parrish on cover of Harper's Bazaar, 1895.
Ill. 139: Cover of Collier's, 1895.

theory (Ill. 136). He learned principles of mathematical balance and harmony.

What all this means is that Parrish was not flying by the seat of his pants. Like Saint Gaudens and MacMonnies, he was rigorously trained in technique.

BREAKTHROUGH YEAR

Parrish's breakthrough year was 1895, when he was twenty-five (cf. Ill. 135). He had his first paid commission and sold his first painting: *Old King Cole and the Fiddlers Three* for the Mask and Wig Club at the University of Pennsylvania (Ill. 137). The colors in this eleven-foot-wide oil painting are subdued and flat: not what we think of as typical Parrish colors. What is like later Parrish are the sharp, intricate outlines and the precise detail. Look at the lace collar on the man playing second fiddle. Such detail is always characteristic of Parrish, no matter what he's painting.

Also in 1895, he created his first magazine cover. Someone who saw *Old King Cole* asked him to submit a cover for *Harper's Bazaar* (Ill. 138). The cover won him national recognition. It turned out that sales jumped every time a Parrish picture was on a cover: lots of people find the world as Parrish sees it very appealing. Parrish was soon in great demand for magazine covers (for example, Ill. 139).

A quick word about the colors of Parrish paintings and reproductions. Illustration 140 is a photograph of an original Parrish painting. Oil paintings are covered with a layer of varnish that yellows and darkens over time. Parrish often painted on Masonite, which tends to warp over time, cracking the varnish and allowing air to alter the colors. Illustration 141 is a painting used on a magazine cover. Color reproductions have a different set of problems. They fade if exposed to the sun, and their colors change if the paper they're printed on turns brown.

For those reasons, even if we're looking at a real print or a real painting, it's difficult to be sure which has colors as Parrish originally painted them. Perhaps neither one does. If we're looking at photos or reproductions online, it's almost impossible to guess what the colors originally were. When looking for photos for this book, I mostly chose the reproductions that had colors similar to the original Parrish paintings that I've seen, and whose colors appealed to me most.

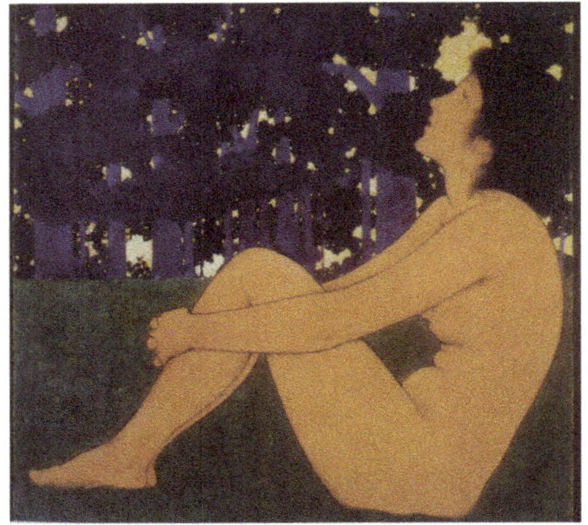

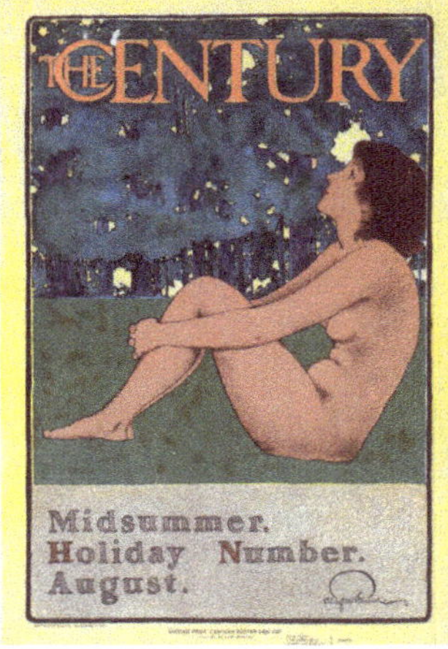

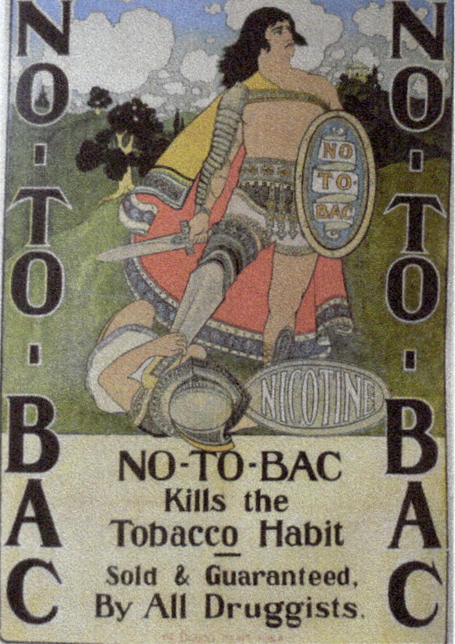

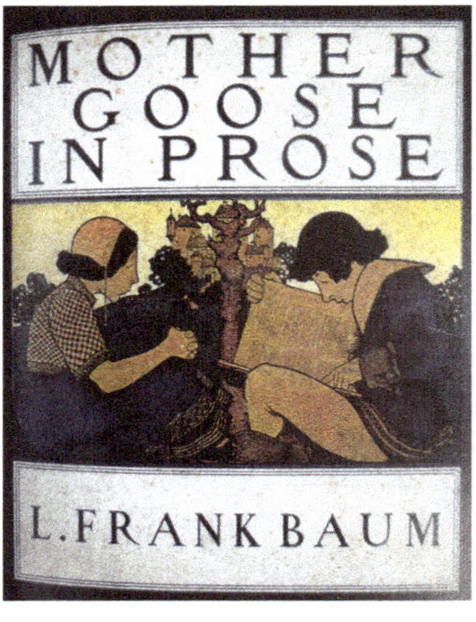

*Ill. 140: Century Magazine, 1897. Ill. 141:Original oil painting of the
Century cover. Ill. 142: Advertisement for No-To-Bac, 1896.
Ill. 143: Cover for Baum's Mother Goose, 1897.*

Parrish was also much in demand for advertisements, and was well paid for them. I love his image of No-To-Bac stomping on Nicotine (Ill. 142).

In the late 1890s, besides large-scale paintings, magazine covers, and advertisements, Parrish also began to do book illustrations. *Mother Goose in Prose,* one of L. Frank Baum's pre-Oz works, was published with Parrish illustrations in 1897 (Ill. 143). Parrish was soon in high demand for book illustrations as well.

EARLY CAREER

In 1898, when he'd been out of college about two years, Parrish moved to Cornish, New Hampshire. An artist's colony had grown up in Cornish after Augustus Saint Gaudens set up his studio there in the 1880s. Parrish's parents were among those who had moved there. In 1898, when he'd been out of college about two years, Parrish also moved to Cornish, where he began constructing a lovely, large home—The Oaks—for himself and his wife.

Then stress kicked in. By the time he was barely thirty, he had achieved national fame. He had deadlines for magazine covers, ads, and books. He had to earn the cost of building a substantial home and cope with all the usual hassles of construction. In 1899, Parrish's parents (those respectable Quakers) separated; his mother moved to a religious commune in southern California.

As many of us know to our dismay, stress can screw up one's immune system. Parrish contracted tuberculosis, which at the time was life-threatening. Around 1900, eight thousand or so New Yorkers were dying annually of tuberculosis. Until antibiotics were discovered, the "cure" for it was a long visit to a warm, dry place.

In 1901, *Century* magazine offered Parrish an assignment: visit to Arizona to illustrate an article on the American Southwest. Arizona didn't become a state until 1912, so this was an exotic assignment. Parrish jumped at the chance to spend time in a warmer climate than New Hampshire (Ill. 144).

The Arizona project was a turning point in his style. He began to use the intense colors he saw in the landscape of the Southwest (Ill. 145-146). This type of color becomes characteristic of Parrish: saturated, vivid, intense.

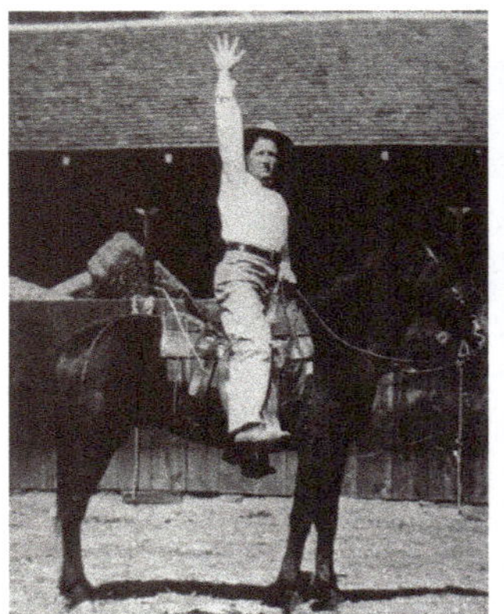
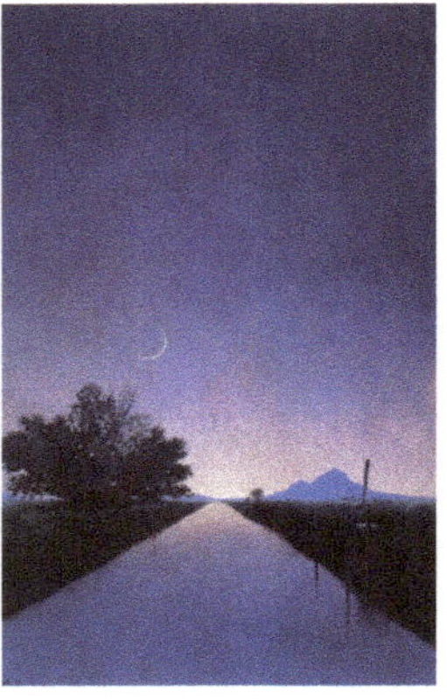
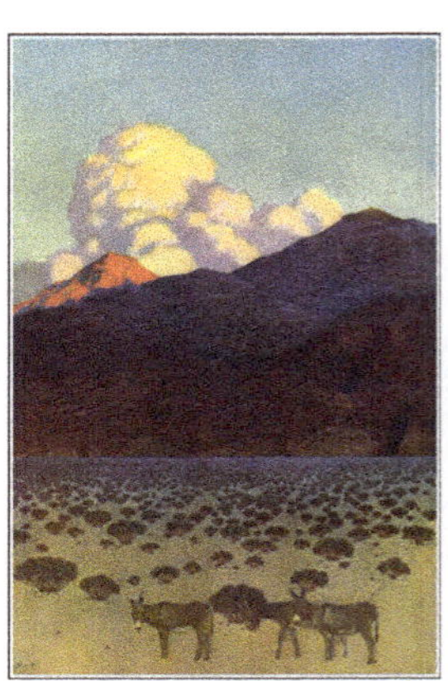
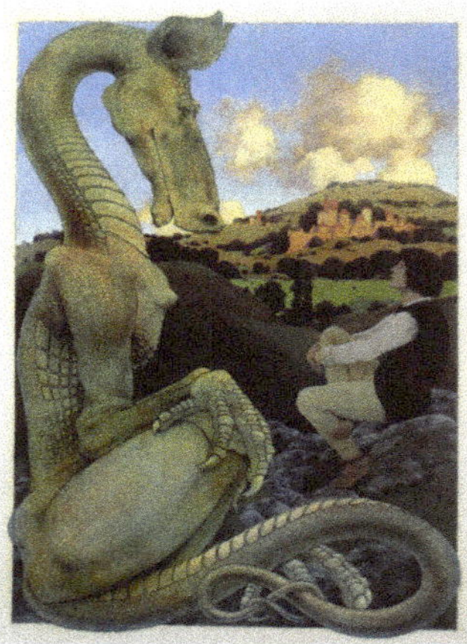
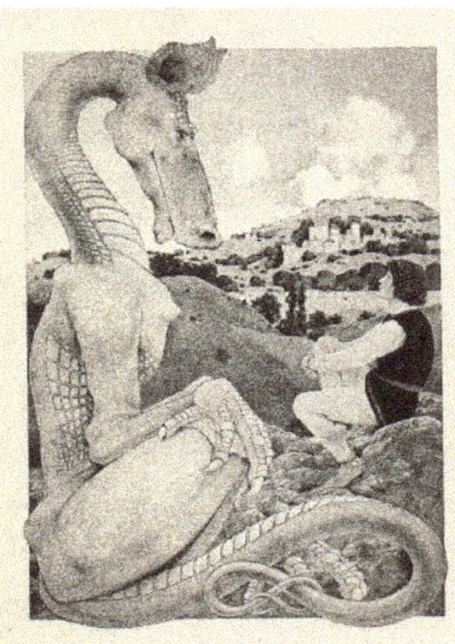
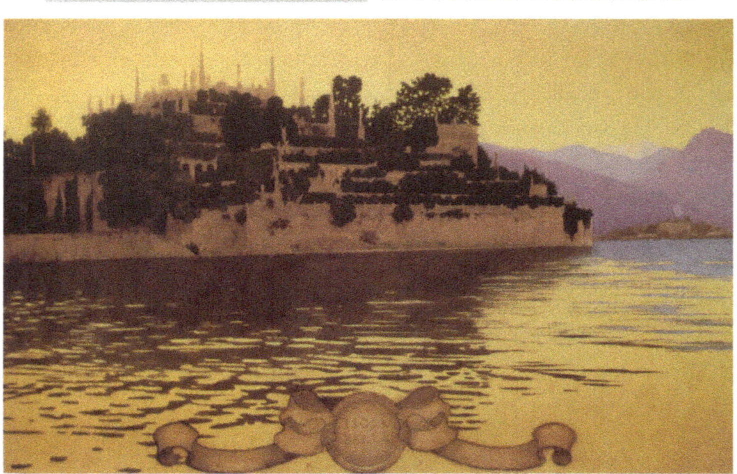

*Ill. 144: Parrish in Arizona, 1902. Ill. 145: Hot Springs Yavapai, 1902.
Ill. 146: Growth in the Desert, 1902. Ill. 147-148: for Kenneth Grahame's
The Reluctant Dragon (in Dream Days), color original and as published,
1902. Ill. 149: for Wharton's Italian Villas, 1904.*

BOOK ILLUSTRATIONS

After he returned from the Southwest, Parrish continued to illustrate books. Kenneth Grahame's *The Golden Age* (1899) and *Dream Days* (1902) were published with Parrish illustrations in New York and London. Although the illustrations were painted in color, they were published in high-quality black and white (Ill. 147-148). The illustrations were acclaimed on both sides of the Atlantic, so Parrish had achieved an international reputation by the time he was thirty-ish.

The first book published with color reproductions of Parrish's work was Edith Wharton's *Italian Villas,* 1904 (Ill. 149). From 1900 to 1910 or so, Parrish did illustrations for many other children's books (Ill. 150-153). Books with Parrish illustrations immediately became favorites of adult collectors as well as children, and he was paid well for illustrating them. The last children's book he illustrated—some say the best—was the *Knave of Hearts,* published in 1923 (Ill. 154-155).

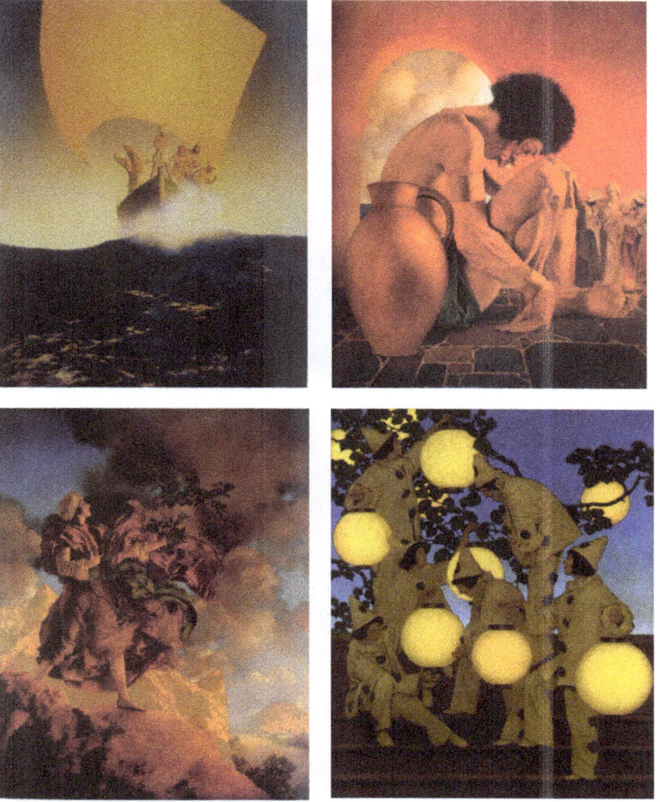

Parrish illustrations for children's books. Ill. 150: History of Codadad and His Brothers, 1906. Ill. 151: Sinbad Plots Against the Giant, 1907. Ill. 152: Princess Parrizade, 1906. Ill. 153: Lantern-Bearers, 1908.

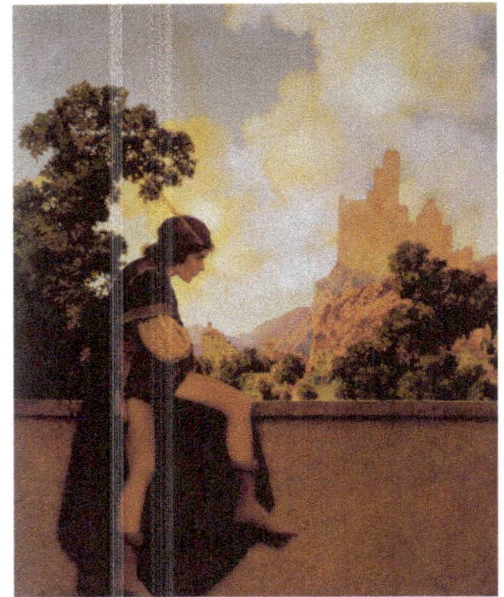
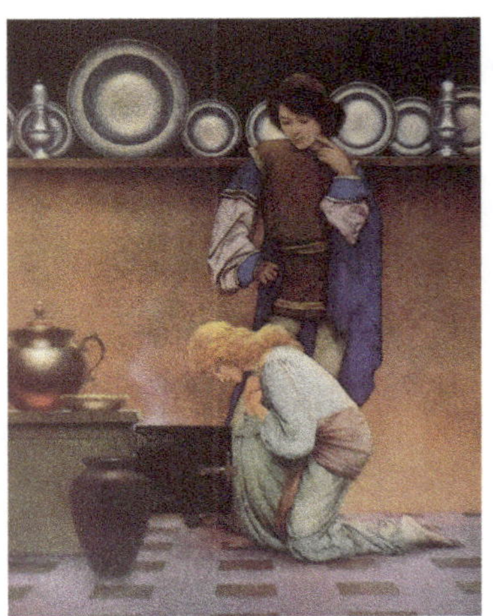
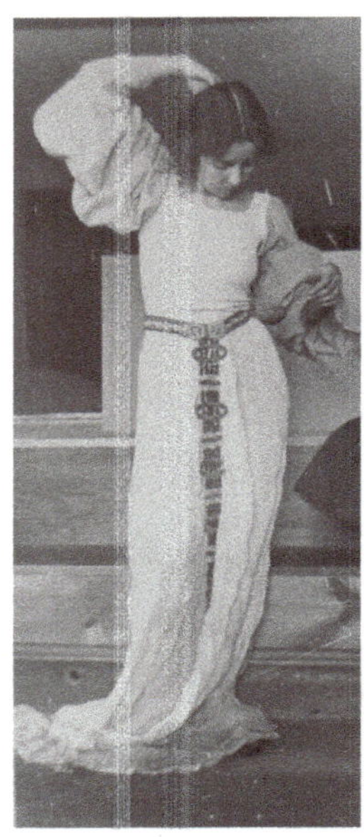
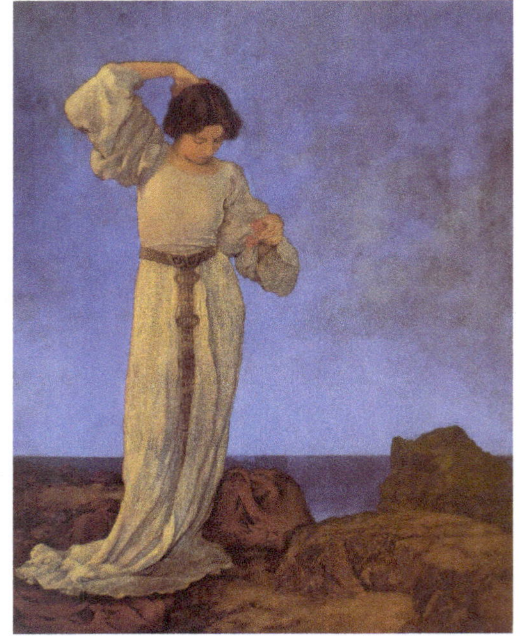

Ill. 154-155: Parrish illustrations for The Knave of Hearts, 1923. Ill. 156: Sue Lewin posing for Griselda, 1910. Ill. 157: Griselda, 1910.

Starting around 1910, Parrish's main model was Sue Lewin. Years later, Parrish said he could tell her: "You are in a large and strange empty hall. You do not know whether there are any lurking murderers waiting beyond the next archway or not." And Sue would strike a suitable pose. Having a model with imagination was invaluable to Parrish.

By the early 1900s, Parrish's works were immediately recognizable: he had a unique combination of style and subject. His figures were elaborately costumed. They're not of any specific time or place, but definitely *not* American in the early twentieth century. The backgrounds are fairy-tale settings: palaces, castles, mountains, the high seas. To show these, he uses dramatic color and lighting. His detail has been called "hyperrealistic"—it looks more real than real.

Related to this is the fact that Parrish relied heavily on photos, many of which survive (Ill. 156-157). For many artists, copying a photo is a sign of a lack of imagination. For Parrish, it was practical—even necessary—due to the way he painted. He often put down a layer of varnish not just as the final coat, but between layers of paint. The extra layers of varnish allow the light to penetrate deeper into his paintings, beneath the surface. It makes them glow. A layer of paint plus varnish might take up to two weeks to dry. After even a few hours, however, it would be difficult to get a live model to strike exactly the same pose and to rearrange all that complex drapery in the same folds. Using a photo was a practical solution to a problem. Parrish is *not* attempting to capture a moment in a naturalistic way.

Also with respect to Parrish's style: he always has a sort of mathematical balance in his compositions. It's not just symmetry, and it's never the same arrangement twice. There is a scientific theory behind this—Parrish learned it at the Academy of Fine Arts—but I don't know the proper terms. I do know that when I tried to crop any of his paintings for inclusion in this book, they always looked very wrong.

So at age thirty-five, Parrish had an unmistakable and unique combination of style and subject, and it was emphatically *not* like mainstream painting in the United States (Ill. 124-134).

PARRISH AS ENTREPRENEUR

By 1905, Parrish had increasing fame and a very comfortable income. But he didn't just settle down to enjoy them.

In 1903, his *Air Castles* won a competition for the cover of the 250th issue of *Ladies Home Journal*. The *Journal* sold prints of the painting, which gave Parrish the idea for a wider distribution of his

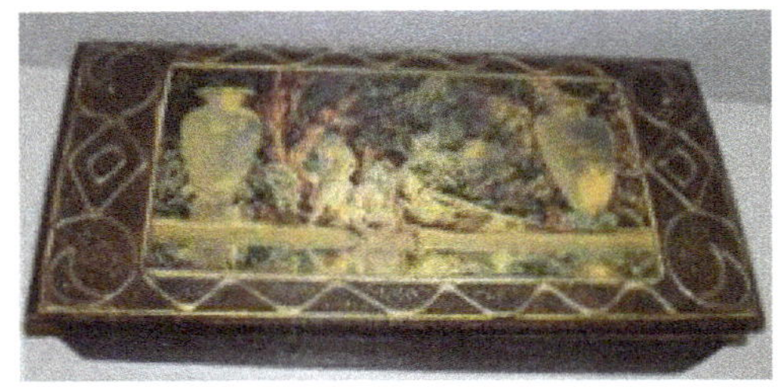

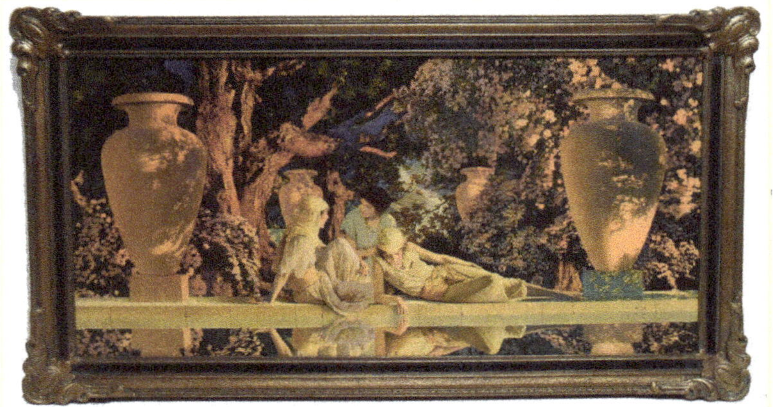

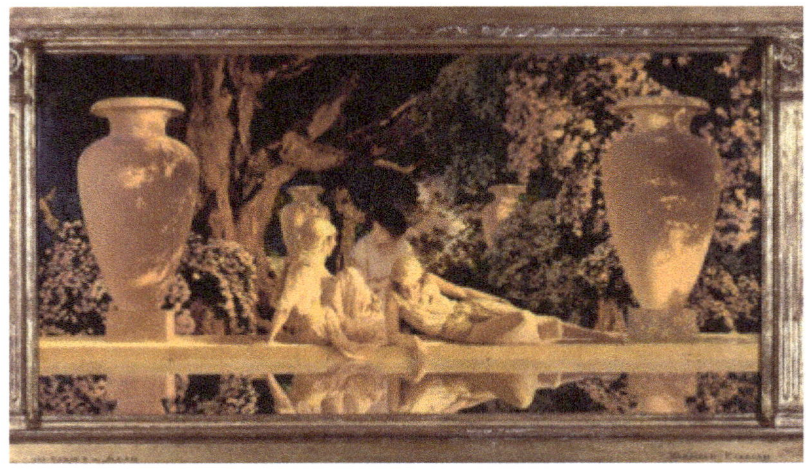

*Parrish, Garden of Allah, 1918. Ill. 158: Candy box. Ill. 159: art print.
Ill. 160: original oil.*

future works. By 1915, forty-five-year-old Parrish had perfected this new business model. The client was given the right to a one-time use of an image, for a magazine cover, book illustration, and so on. The *Garden of Allah* was created as a design for the candy box (Ill. 158). Parrish then sold the right to reproduce prints of the work, in return for royalties (Ill. 159). Finally, Parrish sold the actual painting (Ill. 160). This much financial savvy and efficiency is unusual among artists, even today.

In 1918, Parrish made over $50,000 *just* from royalties on the designs for this and two other candy boxes. That would be almost $1 million in 2019 dollars. Great illustrators such as Howard Pyle and N.C. Wyeth hadn't thought of doing this. Augustus Saint Gaudens and Frederick MacMonnies did something similar by selling smale-scale bronze reproductions of their sculptures—but even small-scale bronzes are only affordable for the upper class and upper-middle-class. On the other hand, anyone could afford a Parrish print.

The business model of selling the original and the rights to mass-produced, low-cost reproductions in exchange for royalties— that was Parrish's creation. It made him wealthy, and also made him one of the most popular and familiar American artists to that time.

Daybreak, painted in 1922, was the first work Parrish created specifically for reproduction as an art print (Ill. 161). Within three years, it was estimated that a reproduction of *Daybreak* was hanging in one out of four American homes. These were voluntary purchases. Clearly

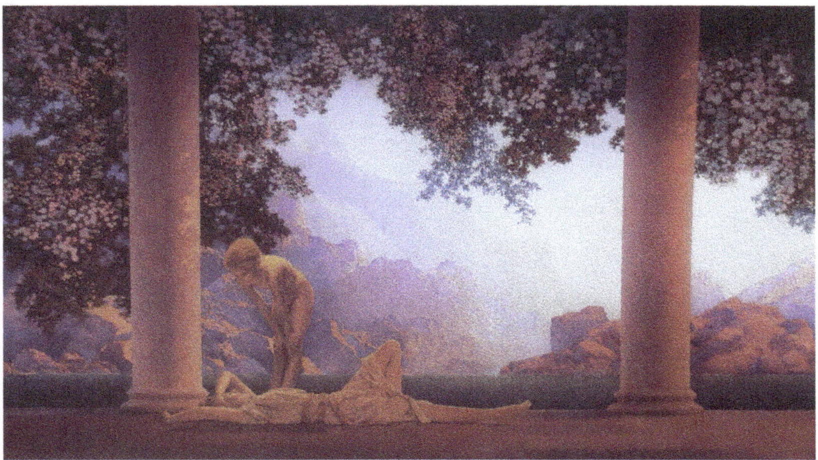

Ill. 161: Parrish, Daybreak, 1922; Wikipedia.

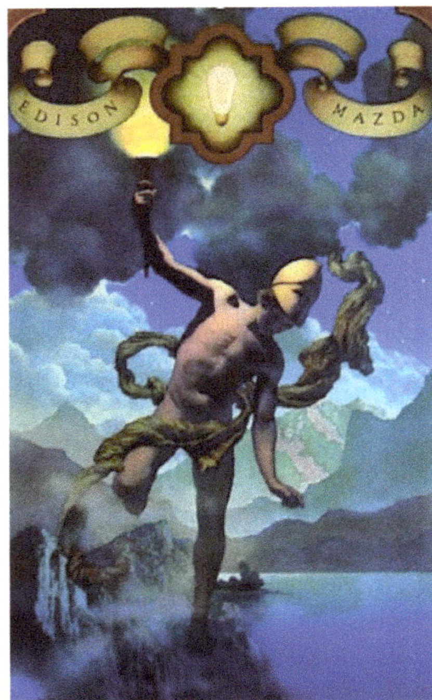

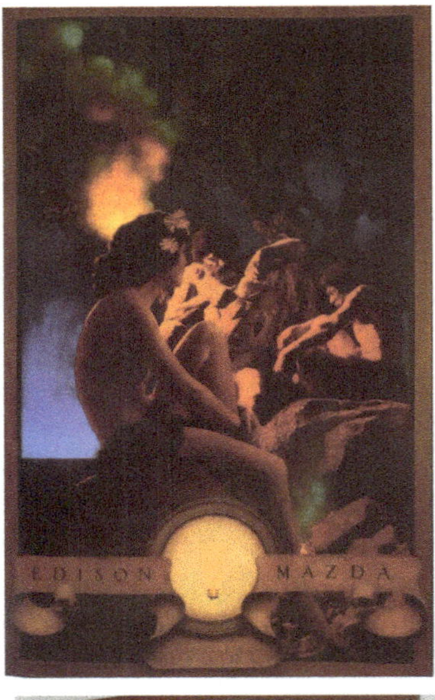

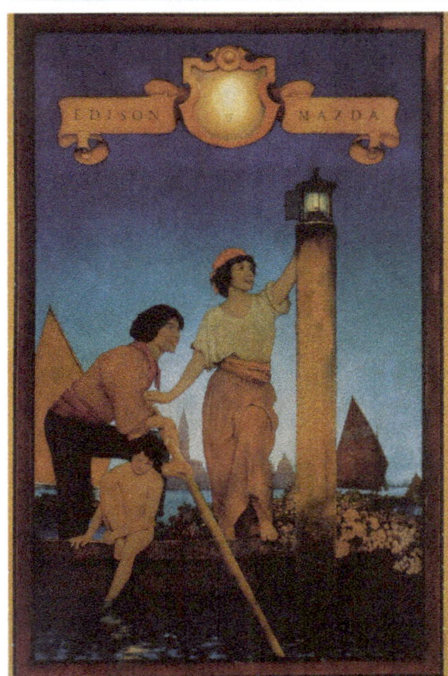

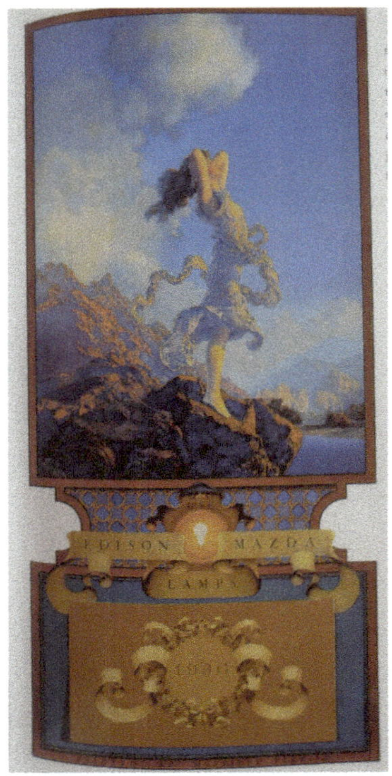

*Some of Parrish's Edison Mazda calendars. Ill. 162: Prometheus, 1920.
Ill. 163: Primitive Man, 1921. Ill. 164: Venetian Lamplighters, 1922.
Ill. 165: Ecstasy, 1929.*

something about Parrish's take on life struck a chord with a lot of people.

Parrish's popularity wasn't confined to a wide distribution of art prints. In 1918, he started creating illustrations for calendars by Edison Mazda, a division of General Electric. These were printed in fourteen-color process, the highest technology of the time for color printing. Their theme was aspects of light, in history or as a natural phenomenon (Ill. 162-165).

Over sixteen years, to 1934, twenty million copies of these calendars were published. It was the first time any artist's work—not just Parrish's—reached such a huge audience. Among the most famous of the Edison Mazda calendars was *Ecstasy*, created in 1929 (Ill. 165). The style is characteristically Parrish: a fairy-tale setting, an exotic costume, hyperrealistic detail, and dramatic, saturated color.

In the years following World War I, Parrish's success at selling prints freed him from the need to create ads or do book illustrations, with the compromises, interruptions, and deadlines those involved. In 1936, *Time* magazine named the three most popular artists in the world, in terms of high-end color prints: Van Gogh, Cezanne, and Parrish.

LATER LIFE

At age 61, most people are thinking of retiring. Parrish said, "The commercial art game ... tempts a man to repeat himself. It's an awful thing to get to be a rubber stamp." He declared that he wouldn't paint any more "girls on rocks." (Quoted in the *American National Biography*.) So in 1931, he switched to painting landscapes.

Years before, Parrish had designed at least one pure landscape. *The Dream Garden* still glows in the lobby of the Curtis Building in Philadelphia (Ill. 166). It's 15 feet high by 49 feet wide, and was executed in favrile glass by Tiffany Studios. Not a shabby start to a career as a landscape artist!

For thirty years after 1931, Parrish painted only landscapes. They have the same crisp detail as all his work since the 1890s, and the same brilliant colors as his work since the trip to the Southwest in 1901. In fact, the colors are sometimes even brighter, perhaps because they don't have to play second fiddle to the figures. There are no fantasy elements, but Parrish was not rendering a naturalistic record of the views from his window. He combined elements from different places. For example, the same oak tree appears in half a dozen paintings, in different settings.

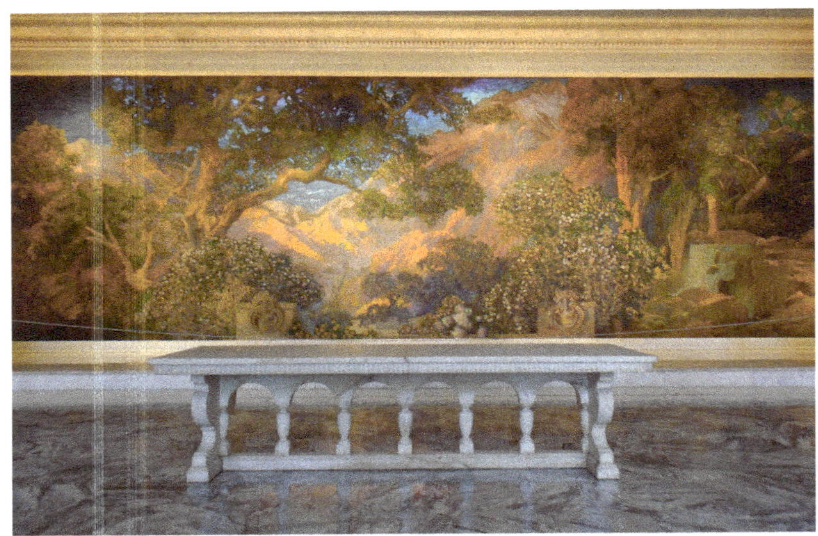

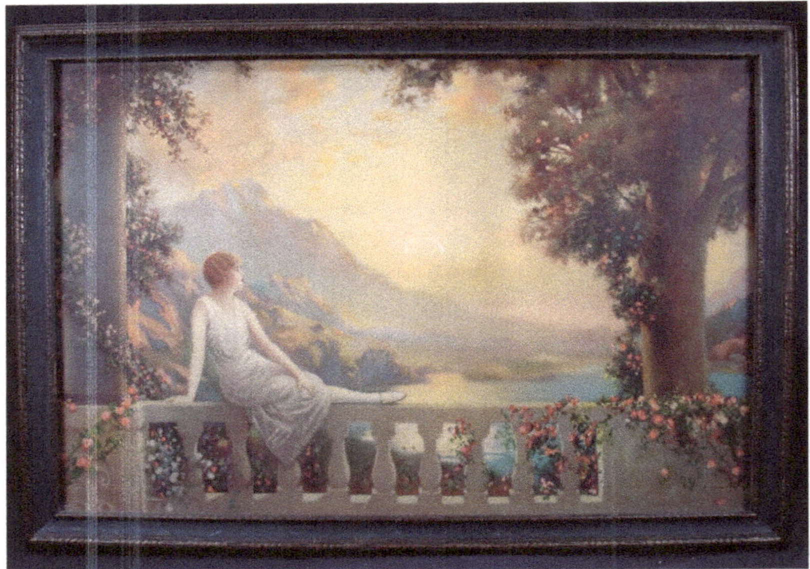

Ill. 166: Parrish, Dream Garden, 1914, Tiffany mosaic landscape in lobby of the Curtis Building, Philadelphia; Smallbones / Wikipedia.
Ill. 167: R. Atkinson Fox (an imitator of Parrish), Sunset Dreams, 1920s or 1930s.

In 1935, Parrish began a series of landscapes for calendars, which he continued for twenty-seven years. The landscapes never sold as well as the "girls on rocks," but they brought him a very comfortable income.

THE ART WORLD IN THE 1950S

Meanwhile, the art world was changing. Parrish's paintings sold well, so there were a lot of imitators. Like most imitators, their works were of much poorer quality (Ill. 167). The colors tended to be insipid pastels. The figures tended to be limp. The lines tended to be kind of fuzzy. But the presence—the ubiquity—of the imitations changed the context of popular art. The style and subject that Parrish had worked in became so prevalent that people could no longer see his works with fresh eyes. It's like looking at last year's fashions, or listening to last year's number one pop hit for the 534th time: it's too familiar to make an impression. Critics started calling such art "coy" and "sentimental".

In the 1950s, art critics began to praise Abstract Expressionism. Clement Greenberg, in a 1939 essay called "Avant-Garde and Kitsch," firmly classified Parrish as kitsch. He condemned Parrish's "hallucinatory high-octane realism" and brushless surface, as contrasted with Pollock or de Kooning. Parrish referred to their works as "scribbles."

In 1961, at age 91, Parrish stopped painting. His final work was *End of Day*. He lived to see the Metropolitan Museum acquire his *Tempest* in 1965. When he died in 1966, at age 96, he was still well off.

PARRISH: EVALUATION

What was Parrish's influence? He has a unique combination of style and subject. That's no small thing for an artist—to be recognizable without using a repetitive gimmick.

Speaking as an art historian, I don't think Parrish made any innovations that will have repercussions for the future history of art. But he did have a strong influence in some areas. Children's book illustration and the fantasy landscapes on sci-fi novels both owe a lot to Parrish (Ill. 169-170; compare Ill. 168).

Perhaps more importantly, he created a business model—selling the rights for reproduction, then selling the original—that's still in use by financially savvy artists.

What about Parrish's attitude—his sense of life? He didn't have a pampered, protected existence. Parrish lived through two world wars, the Korean War, and the start of the Cold War. He had life-threatening

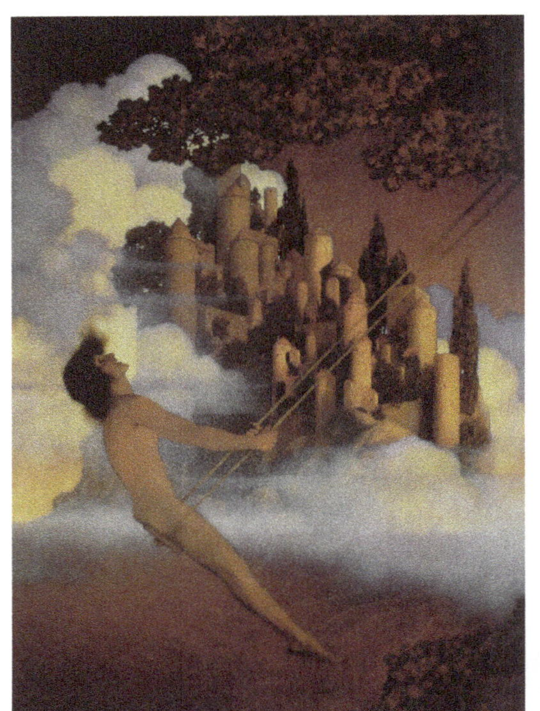

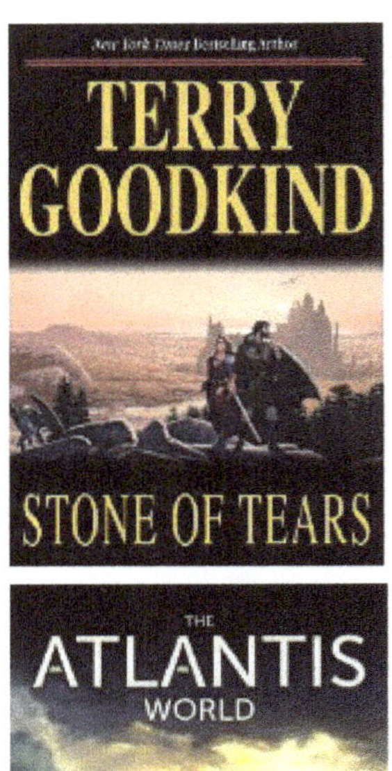

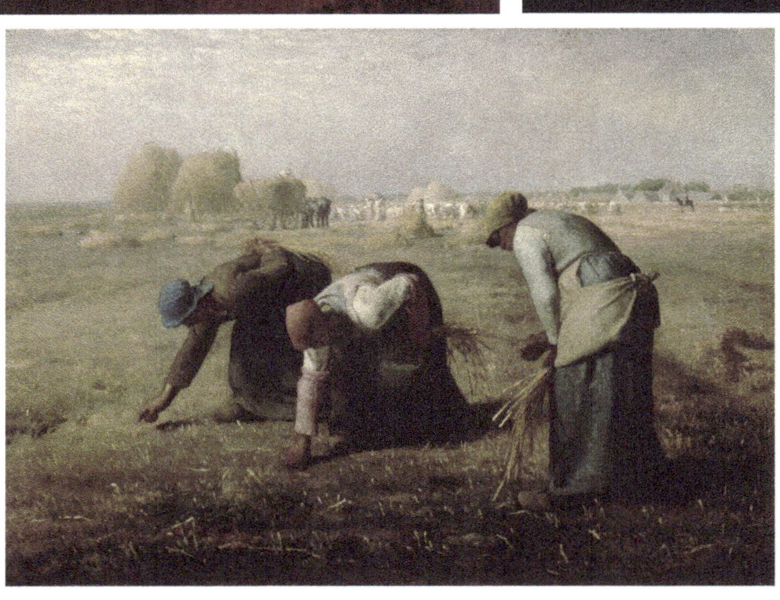

Ill. 168: Parrish, Dinky Bird, 1904; Wikipedia. Ill. 169-170:
Covers of books by Goodkind and Riddle.
Ill. 171: Millet, Gleaners, 1857; Wikipedia.

bouts with typhoid and tuberculosis. His parents split up and he grew away from his wife. Yet Parrish consistently shows figures who are happy or thoughtful. Even in landscapes, where no figures appear, the world looks like a beautiful place where people can be happy.

The best illustration of this is in contrasting images rather than words. Millet's *Gleaners,* 1857, shows farm workers bowed down, concentrating on the ground (Ill. 171). All the figures are below the horizon. The sky is gray and cold, the colors dull. In *Harvest,* 1905, Parrish shows a farm worker standing upright and looking into the distance from the top of a hill, in the midst of a gorgeous sunset (Ill. 172).

It takes a lot of time to paint, especially in the detail in which Parrish used. In practical terms—because a lifetime is finite—that means artists usually paint what's most important to them. This uplifting, benevolent view of life recurs again and again in Parrish's works. That's the way he sees the world.

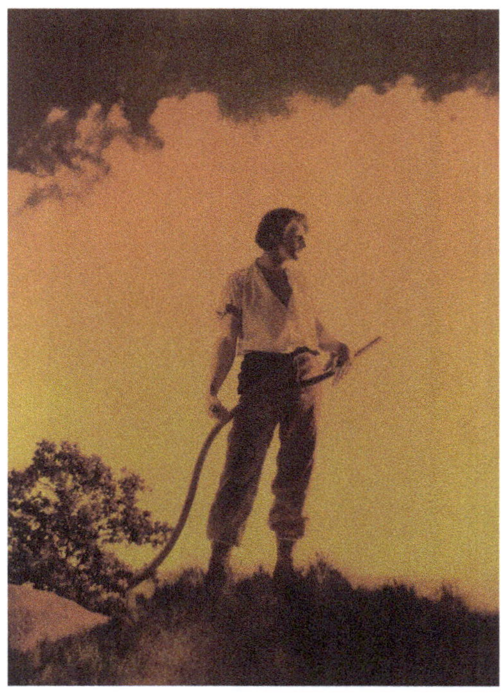

Ill. 172: Parrish, Harvest, 1905.

CHAPTER 5
Give Me More!

Where art is concerned, no slide is as good as the real thing. If you like the works of Saint Gaudens, MacMonnies, and/or Parrish, go find some to see in person! Between them they've created hundreds of works. Chances are there's one near you. Also search the artists' names on DianneDuranteWriter.com. I continually add new essays.

WORKS BY SAINT GAUDENS

SIRIS: Search "Saint Gaudens" as artist on the Smithsonian Institution's Inventory of Art (https://siris-artinventories.si.edu/ipac20/ipac.jsp?profile=ariall). It will give you a list of all his works nationwide, outdoors and in museums.

New York City: here's a list of outdoor sculptures by Saint Gaudens.
- *Farragut*, 1880: Madison Square Park
- *David Stewart Memorial*, 1883, Green-Wood Cemetery, Brooklyn
- *Richard Randall*, 1884: Sailors' Snug Harbor, Staten Island
- *Peter Cooper*, 1897: Cooper Union
- *Sherman Monument*, 1903: Fifth Avenue at 59th Street
- Busts of Sherman and Lincoln, 1900 and 1905, at Bronx Hall of Fame of Great Americans

Metropolitan Museum of Art: The MMA has a couple dozen of Saint Gaudens's works, including several of his early cameos, the Bryant Vase, bas-relief portraits of Cornelius Vanderbilt, Robert Louis Stevenson, and many others, and reductions of *Diana, Puritan, Victory* (from *Sherman*), and *Lincoln*. Search MetMuseum.org to find out which are on display and which gallery they're in.

Saint Gaudens National Historical Park: the artist's home in Cornish, with a wonderful collection of his works.

WORKS BY MACMONNIES

<u>SIRIS</u>: Search "MacMonnies" as artist on the Smithsonian Institution's Inventory of Art (<u>https://siris-artinventories.si.edu/ipac20/ipac.jsp?profile=ariall</u>). It'll give you a list of all his works nationwide, outdoors and in museums.

New York City: here's a list of outdoor sculptures by MacMonnies.
- *Nathan Hale*, 1890: City Hall Park.
- *James S.T. Stranahan*, 1891: Prospect Park.
- Bowery Savings Bank pediment, 1894: 130 Bowery.
- Angels on the Washington Arch, 1894: Washington Square Park.
- Angels at St. Paul the Apostle, 1897: Church of St. Paul the Apostle, Columbus Ave. at 59th St.
- *Horse Tamers*, 1898: Prospect Park.
- Soldiers' and Sailors' Arch (groups of Army and Navy and chariot on top), 1901: Grand Army Plaza, Brooklyn.
- *General Henry Warner Slocum*, 1905: Grand Army Plaza.
- *Truth* and *Beauty*, 1920: New York Public Library, Fifth Avenue at 42nd St.
- *Civic Virtue*, 1922: Green-Wood Cemetery.
- Busts of John Lothrop Motley, 1910; James McNeill Whistler, 1930; Thomas Hastings, 1933; and Simon Newcomb, 1935, all at Bronx Hall of Fame of Great Americans.

<u>Metropolitan Museum of Art</u>: The MMA has his bronze *Bacchante and Infant Faun*, reductions of his *Diana* and *Nathan Hale*, several charming garden sculptures, and a number of his paintings and drawings. Search their site (MetMuseum.org) for information.

<u>Galleries</u>: reductions of works by MacMonnies sometimes come up for sale. Try Conner-Rosenkranz and the Gerald Peters Gallery, both in Manhattan. Even if you can't afford to buy, you can visit.

WORKS BY PARRISH

<u>SIRIS</u>: Search "Parrish" as artist on the Smithsonian Institution's Inventory of Art (<u>https://siris-artinventories.si.edu/ipac20/ipac.jsp?profile=ariall</u>). It'll give you a list of all his works nationwide.

<u>On public view in New York</u>: The bar in the St. Regis Hotel at 2 East Fifty-Fifth Street has Parrish's *Old King Cole.* This large painting was executed in 1906 for John Jacob Astor's Knickerbocker Hotel, at Forty-Second and Broadway. It was said that Parrish was paid $50,000 for it, which would be about $1.3 million today. In 1935, after the Knickerbocker was torn down, it was moved to the St. Regis.

<u>American Illustrators Gallery</u>: 18 East Seventy-Seventh Street. They usually have six or eight works by Parrish on hand, as well as a wonderful collection of works by other illustrators from the same period, including Leyendecker (one of my favorites) and Rockwell.

<u>National Museum of American Illustration</u>: Newport, Rhode Island. It has some spectacular works by Parrish and other ilustrators. Laurence and Judy Cutler run the American Illustrators Gallery and the NMAI.

<u>Metropolitan Museum</u>: still owns only one Parrish painting, his *Tempest.* It also owns a few dozen drawings and prints, seldom on view.

<u>Philadelphia</u>: In Parrish's home town, you can visit *Dream Garden,* the Parrish landscape in Tiffany's favrile glass, in the Curtis Building (601-45 Walnut Street). Call to check the hours and make sure there's not an event scheduled in the space.

<u>Books</u>: Books with Parrish illustrations often appear on the antiquarian market. Try <u>ViaLibri.net</u> to see what's available.

ABOUT THE AUTHOR

At age seven, I won my first writing award: a three-foot-long fire truck with an ear-splitting siren. I've been addicted to writing ever since. As an independent researcher, freelance writer, and lecturer, I indulge my curiosity and share my delight in a variety of topics.

Recent art-related books include *Innovators in Sculpture* and *Innovators in Painting,* and *Getting More Enjoyment from Sculpture You Love.* Sam Roberts in the *New York Times* called my *Outdoor Monuments of Manhattan* (New York University Press, 2007) "a perfect walking-tour accompaniment to help New Yorkers and visitors find, identify and better appreciate statues famous and obscure."

I post art-related material regularly on YouTube and Instagram, and send out three or four weekly recommendations to my mailing list. In 2022, I published two collections of favorites from the Sunday Recommendations: *Starry Solitudes* and *Sunny Sundays.* To join the list, visit https://diannedurantewriter.com/sunday-recommendations.

In the realm of history, I've published *Central Park: The Early Years, Timeline 1900-2021,* and five volumes on Alexander Hamilton: *Alexander Hamilton: A Brief Biography; Alexander Hamilton: A Friend to America,* volumes 1-2; *Alexander Hamilton and the Reynolds Affair;* and *Financial Programs of Alexander Hamilton.*

My website, DianneDuranteWriter.com, has hundreds of posts on sculpture (especially outdoor sculpture in New York City), painting, Central Park, and favorite works from museums. For an up-to-date list of my books, talks, and videos, visit DianneDuranteWriter.com/books-essays.